Jami –

Thank you for being such a dear friend and constant supporter. That's the essence of leadership.

Love you!

Laurie

The
Leadership
Habit

Tammy R. Berberick
Peter Lindsay
Katie Fritchen

The Leadership Habit

Transforming Behaviors to Drive Results

WILEY

For general information about our other products and services, please contact our Customer Care Department within the United States at (800) 762–2974, outside the United States at (317) 572–3993 or fax (317) 572–4002.

Wiley publishes in a variety of print and electronic formats and by print-on-demand. Some material included with standard print versions of this book may not be included in e-books or in print-on-demand. If this book refers to media such as a CD or DVD that is not included in the version you purchased, you may download this material at http://booksupport.wiley.com. For more information about Wiley products, visit www.wiley.com.

ISBN 978–1–119–36320–0 (cloth)
ISBN 978–1–119–36322–4 (ePub)
ISBN 978–1–119–36321–7 (ePDF)

Printed in the United States of America

10 9 8 7 6 5 4 3 2 1

CONTENTS

INTRODUCTION

*T*he *Leadership Habit* provides the framework for patterns of behavior that will transform the way you lead. The book is both a leadership resource and a call to action. It asserts that leaders who form daily habits in 10 key areas will be more successful in developing productive teams and in building long-term professional and personal growth. Organizations thrive best when leaders (1) drive for results, (2) build the right teams, (3) influence others, (4) understand the business, (5) execute vision, (6) encourage excellence, (7) develop positive relationships, (8) develop customer focus, (9) foster innovation, and (10) model personal growth.

Leading can be a strenuous mental and physical activity. Deciding on higher performance and excellence is a mental commitment to discover or rediscover how to lead and a physical commitment to do something to create the change. Developing the leadership habit takes time and daily practice.

One differentiating characteristic of skilled leaders is the willingness to reflect on and reshape behaviors to accomplish more. In flight, an error of only a few degrees can determine whether the aircraft arrives safely at its destination. Leadership, however, is a delicate relationship between knowing the destination and setting the right course to get there; and correction should be a regular part of leading. Adjusting, adapting, and trying new things enable leaders to arrive on time and on target.

Among other things, books, videos and multimedia presentations, development programs, and the experiences of others can influence the habits that make leaders effective. However, reading, studying, hearing, or watching—although insightful—are ultimately insufficient. Leadership habits are formed by consistently doing smart leadership behaviors. Applying good ideas transforms behaviors to drive results. Subtle differences in the ways leaders act and respond, little differences in the ways they behave, can make a big difference in their results.

Through case studies and global research that looked at the capacity and potential of modern managers to lead their teams to excellence, Crestcom International evolves tools to help leaders achieve higher performance through team and individual development. As managers grow their skills to lead teams, projects, and initiatives, they find answers to problems and create new pathways for team success.

The experience of developing leadership teams in over 60 countries worldwide has validated two important leadership lessons. The first lesson suggests that leaders need knowledge of new business ideas, new technologies, and new management tools. The second lesson is foundational and crucial for managers to reach their potential and achieve higher results. Leaders must practice and immediately apply the new knowledge obtained and feel the positive impact of their actions. This application, refinement, and broader perspective of insight never ends.

Leading is its own language. At last count, there are roughly five thousand languages spoken in the world today, and the language that crosses all borders, cultures, industry types, and sizes of organizations is the language of results-driven leadership. The language of leaders is not limited to words but instead to the ways leaders communicate through actions to achieve the results they want. Managers from diverse organizations who have completed Crestcom International's leadership development program now speak the same leadership language, no matter where they are located. Although they may have different perspectives or unique business or organizational expectations, managers around the world are generally unified in their desires to grow themselves and develop others. Growth and development occurs as managers learn and apply indispensable skills for leading.

The Leadership Habit illustrates the unifying effect of a common leadership language that drives profit and progress with leaders around the world. Crestcom International provides structured leadership development on a global scale. Representatives, faculty, and facilitators of Crestcom dot the globe, and they have contributed greatly to the collective wisdom of this book. The stories in the book are based on the experiences of professionals who have invested in Crestcom programs for leadership development. By turning core global leadership methods into local training for leadership teams, Crestcom trainers help all organizations speak a common language of leadership that every person can comprehend. We want everyone to be fluent in the language of leadership.

With a structured approach, managers can translate the words in this book into a language of leadership habits, attitudes, and actions. Leaders committed to building strong teams deliberately create experiences for themselves and others to learn and apply skills that will lift more than an organization's financials. The development of managers into effective leaders has the potential to enlarge the productivity of every employee, as well as clients, suppliers, and partners eager to promote your brand or purpose. The improvement of yourself and of your team depends on how well you develop habits in 30 specific skill areas presented here, along with actionable ideas from leaders for leaders.

Make leadership your habit.

ACKNOWLEDGMENTS

This book is dedicated to the many Crestcom licensees, facilitators, faculty, representatives, and staff who have chosen to dedicate their lives to making the world a better place by developing stronger, more ethical leaders across the world. Thank you for your endless passion, excellence, and continuous innovation.

We appreciate the Crestcom International faculty members and Crestcom licensees who helped us by contributing their stories, experiences, ideas, and content that made this book possible.

Crestcom International Faculty

Amanda Gore	Lisa A. Ford
Amy Lynch	Marcia Steele
Andy Bounds	Mark Sanborn
Bob Johnson	Dr. Nido Qubein
Colleen Stanley	Patricia Fripp
George Walther	Robert "Bob" Pike
Harvey Mackay	Roger Dawson
Jack Mackey	Ron Crossland
Jim Cathcart	Simon Bailey
Dr. Jim Hennig	Dr. Terry Paulson
John Hersey	Thomas Frey
Dr. John Tickell	Tom Hopkins
Dr. Kimberly Alyn	Zig Ziglar

Contributing Crestcom Licensees

Alfonso Contreras, Chile

Anurag Sharma, India

Arnd Meyer-Hermenau, Germany

Charles Mullenders, France

Dave Strathmann, United States

David Bell, Thailand

Estelle Miller, Canada

Heather Rosenfeld, United States

Heidi Achong, Costa Rica

Hisham Dabbagh, Kingdom of Saudi
   Arabia

Hoàng Ngọc Bích, Vietnam

Ingrid Martinez, Dominican
   Republic

Jack Neeway, United States

Jamie Lord, Australia

John Reeb, United States

Lakshmi Vasan, India

Naresh Shotham, India

Rajendra Muthye, India

Ram Ramesh, Trinidad & Tobago

Renata Tulsie, Trinidad & Tobago

Wolfgang Struensee, Germany

This book presents unique insights into the comprehensive subject matter demanded by organization leaders who invest in transforming managers into leaders. Although many of the stories shared within are based on actual events in Crestcom International's global leadership study and interactive training, character identities, locations, or timelines have been changed or may be composites for purposes of privacy and application simplicity.

Drives for Results

O n Monday, the 29th of October 2012, the city of Manhattan in New York lost electrical power from the disastrous consequences of a hurricane. With unceasing rain, the lower floors and elevator shafts of New York University's Langone Medical Center flooded. As the wind and rain shook the windows of the hospital, seven nurses who staffed the neonatal intensive care unit on the ninth floor of the hospital showed how a team can be driven for results.

Their results were not measured in profitability or common performance metrics, but in saving the delicate lives of 20 tiny babies. When the backup generators failed, the seven nurses with shared focus did what might have appeared impossible.

All of the infant ventilators and critically essential equipment stopped, triggering emergency alarms. The hospital was dangerously dark from the loss of power. The 4-hour battery backups for the babies in the intensive care unit activated, and the countdown began.

The nurses did three critical things: First, they accepted the responsibility and accountability for the life-or-death outcome. Second, they asked the right questions. Third, they decided on a rapid response.

Using the flashlight features on their cellphones, some of the nurses cast light on the isolettes while the others worked furiously to warmly wrap each baby. As they worked, the call came to evacuate the babies, beginning with those with the most severe risk of death.

One by one, each baby was removed from his or her ventilator and carried through the dark, down nine flights of stairs, and out into the fury of the hurricane. Unable to breathe on their own, the babies needed more than evacuation. Nurses had to breathe for each baby throughout the evacuation by manually squeezing a bag to administer oxygen to the baby's lungs.

Four or more people closely attended each baby and nurse, monitoring vital signs as they made their harrowing evacuation in the pitch blackness.

The team synchronized every movement on the stairs by audibly shouting "Step . . . Step . . . Step!" They coordinated every breath. When the team finally emerged from the dark hospital with a baby, a line of ambulances waited. Up and down, the team of nurses and emergency personnel went in this manner until each of the 20 babies was removed from the flooding hospital and placed in a safe one miles from the raging storm. Not one baby died that night.

The courageous example of these seven nurses puts in perspective the capacity of professionals to achieve. While unparalleled in heroism, the intensive care nurses modeled a core competency of leadership—driven for results.

Employees do not really care about the **stated** mission and values of your organization. What they care about is how the mission and values come to life in what they do every day. Mission is a wall decoration without execution and results. The why and the what must be reinforced daily to drive employee ownership and achievement. Employees need to understand the importance of what they are doing, how they contribute, and why it is personal.

> Do your employees own the results of the projects and initiatives assigned to them? Do they own and drive for results, or do they merely go through the motion of effort?

Achieving results that create value for your organization and for your clients requires a commitment to execution at every level. All team members need to internalize accountability and responsibility for the results of projects and initiatives assigned to them. Leaders need to be able to ask the right questions to make good decisions that align with the overall strategic direction of the organization. And everyone needs to be held responsible for tracking and measuring his or her goals to ensure that desired results are attained and obstacles cleared away.

> What is your tracking mechanism for your department's goals?

Accountability

When people are accountable for their own decisions, work, and results, the effectiveness of an organization greatly increases. Of the three keys to driving for results, accountability has the power to lift your whole team to higher performance. Holding yourself and others accountable for decisions, actions, timeliness, and quality differentiates a winning team from an average or failing one.

The successes and dilemmas associated with managing reservoirs provides an analogy for leaders to consider when assigning expectations to groups or individuals.

Communities and regions depend on reservoirs as a source of water but also in some instances for flood control. Constructed with dams, reservoirs collect water from rivers, streams, rain, or melting snow and ice. Engineers design reservoirs to operate at peak capacity, to be full of water most of the time. When water exceeds the capacity of a reservoir, the excess water is typically released slowly to ensure that the operation can continue efficiently.

Water released from a reservoir generates energy by passing through turbines. That is, the balance between holding and releasing water affects the energy created.

Leaders who drive for results also need the energy that comes from channeling others through monitored and measured deliverables. As accountability becomes a routine part of workplace processes, on-time and quality execution generate energy for the whole team and organization.

Available water matters most when producing electricity through turbines. Although people might assume that hydroelectric dams always have adequate reservoir water, engineering depends on rivers, streams, rain, and melt to keep a reservoir full to capacity. The steady outflow and evaporation from a reservoir can deplete the water unless the feeders continue to fill the lake.

Leaders also must regulate the intake and outflow of production expectations on a team. This starts by setting realistic production expectations for employees, and then holding them accountable to hitting those expectations. Without realistic consideration for their capacities or time, it is possible that employees will become drained. The role of leaders who drive for results is to first set realistic levels of output and then monitor and measure workflow to manage the demands placed on employees.

When your expectations exceed the capacity of your team to execute, accountability and responsibility break down and may fail. If your team feels as though there is no hope for being able to achieve the results you are driving, the system may begin to shut down. Water management and team or project management, however, efficiently produce electricity when the balance is right.

In the spring of 1983, the Glen Canyon Dam located upstream from the iconic Grand Canyon in the American Southwest nearly burst. An overwhelming amount of snow and ice melt from the mountains pushed water levels higher than the capacity of the dam. The flood almost changed the face of the Colorado River below the reservoir. Facing the threat of an overtopping situation, the U.S. Bureau of Reclamation and dam managers opened the spillway tunnels to allow as much water through as possible. At the same time, they extended the height of the dam by installing plywood flashboards to increase reservoir holding capacity. As the water continued to rise, the crew at Glen Canyon Dam began to feel vibrations that turned into rumblings, and eventually becoming loud barrages, like a salvo of exploding military shells. The new spillways were failing quite dramatically, as the water rushing through had torn the interior cement walls, throwing rubble and debris out the other end of the dam, into the Colorado River. Had the dam completely failed, the sudden release of over 27 million acre feet of water would have been catastrophic for down-river systems, other dams, and residential areas. Fast action from engineers who constructed the emergency walls helped avert a disaster.

Plywood walls will not prevent the collapse of productivity on teams, but leaders who skillfully engineer teams and individuals to account for activities and accept responsibility can avoid some major productivity problems. By having a strong, transparent framework for regular two-way communication about task or project scope, timelines, and resources, a manager is more likely to keep employees engaged and in flow.

Leaders who *Drive for Results* manage the tension between inspecting the daily or weekly execution of project plans and giving autonomy to team members to fully inspect their own work, stepping up to project completion. Individuals may require differing levels of supervision, but the accountability framework for all employees becomes stronger the more managers empower others to make decisions and drive results for themselves.

The pitfalls that can exist when teams and individuals are not accountable for owning projects, or executing steps to completion, can be expressed in a comical report about four people named Everybody, Anybody, Somebody, and Nobody.

There was an important project, and Everybody was sure that Somebody would do it. Anybody could have done it, but Nobody did it. Somebody got angry about that because it was Everybody's job. Everybody thought that Anybody could do it, but Nobody realized that Everybody wouldn't do it. It ended up that Everybody blamed Somebody when Nobody did what Anybody could have done.

Holding others accountable is an essential practice for leaders who expect to achieve results, but also for peers and coworkers. However, whether you hold yourself accountable can motivate or demotivate others to make and keep commitments. **Managers who hold employees accountable but neglect to hold themselves accountable can derail team or individual motivation needed to drive projects to completion.**

People are naturally more inclined to be accountable when united with the manager by a clear vision of the results and potential impact of their contributions. By first inspiring others to see the bigger picture, leaders may participate in creating urgency, energy, and focus to also ensure that results are achieved on schedule and with quality. Leaders should hold themselves accountable for painting that picture. Otherwise, employees who know the task, but not the purpose, may be indifferent to project expectations and timelines driven from the top. Inspiring employees to personally invest in the success of new initiatives often can be achieved by including them, even in little ways, in the decision-making process and in establishing expectations and timelines.

At its core, **accountability is about integrity**. A chief executive officer (CEO) was getting ready to retire in six months and needed to find a successor. The organization would typically go outside of the organization to bring in a new CEO. But he decided he was going to promote from within; he wanted to give his young executives the opportunity. He gathered them together in the boardroom and said, "I'm going to give one of you the opportunity to be the next CEO." Jim, a young vice president who had been diligently working his way up the corporate ladder, was sitting in the back of the room excited by the news!

The CEO could see the group getting eager and said, "Not so fast. I'm going to give you a project first. You're going to work on it for six months, and then we're going to come back together, and I'm going to see how well you've accomplished the project."

The CEO left the room for a moment and returned with a handful of seeds. He gave each executive in the room one seed and explained, "I want you to take this home and plant it. I want you to water it and take great care of it. In six months, we're going to come back together and look at your progress."

Jim went home that afternoon and anxiously told his wife the whole story. When he finished explaining he asked her, "Don't you have a friend that owns a nursery?" To which she replied, "Yes, I do." He said, "Let's go visit her."

Together, they went to the nursery where their friend gave them all her best suggestions for growing the plant. They bought the best soil and compost, a pot to put it in with good drainage, and she helped them decide the exact spot by a window that would provide the best light. After returning home, Jim planted the seed.

A few weeks passed, and nothing at all had changed with the seed. Frustrated, Jim exclaimed, "I don't think your friend knows what she's talking about!" His wife responded, "Let's give it some more time." A few more fretful weeks went by and still nothing!

So, Jim got on the computer and searched for other nurseries and advice on germination and growing plants. He found a very expensive specialty organization based in another country, and he imported new soil and new fertilizer to transplant his seed. A few more weeks went by and *still* nothing! By that point, everyone at the office was bragging about how great their plants looked, and he was feeling very discouraged.

The 6-month check-in meeting arrived, and it was time for the evaluation. Poor Jim did not get a single sprout. He took his plant—his pot filled with soil—to the office and tried to hide it in the back corner, behind all the other beautiful, healthy plants. The CEO walked into the boardroom and started looking at each potted plant. "Wow! These are amazing. Look at how big that one is! Impressive! Who did this one?"

He spotted Jim's pot in the very back with nothing but dirt and asked, "Who's plant is this?" Hesitantly, yet clearly, Jim stepped forward and said, "That would be me. That's my plant." Sternly, the CEO replied, "Jim, I need you to come up here." Jim walked up to the front of the boardroom with his empty pot, and he could feel his face turn red. His pulse pounded in his ears. The CEO then asked, "What happened?"

Jim despondently explained, "I don't know. I tried so hard. My wife has a friend who owns a nursery. We followed her advice. I even bought exotic soil and fertilizer that was shipped to me from another country. I tried everything and got nothing. I'm very sorry I failed."

At that moment, the CEO turned him around to the group and declared, "Ladies and gentlemen, your next CEO!" A collective gasp went out as Jim's peers were shocked. "What! Why? Because he said he failed? Okay, well I failed before," one of his coworkers responded.

The CEO explained, "No. That's not why. It's because six months ago, when we first came together, I handed each of you a boiled seed. None of you should have been able to grow a plant from the seed I gave you. Jim was the only one who chose to do the right thing even if it cost him a promotion. That's the kind of person I want to lead this organization."

When you sow honesty with accountability, you will reap prosperity.

Many leaders cite a lack of accountability among their staff members and direct reports as a key issue affecting their organization. Poor accountability is often triggered by lack of clear expectations and roles. As the leader, it is your responsibility to communicate roles and desired outcomes. Help others accept responsibility by communicating with them, not to them.

How do you ensure accountability?

Start by answering these questions. Do all projects and initiatives have:

- A goal—what does winning look like?
- One clear owner?
- A project plan with dates, deliverables, and a point person for each deliverable?
- A standard check-in process for deliverables?

Holding yourself accountable as the leader can help you achieve results besides demonstrating your integrity. Aanya, the manager of accounts of a leading biochemical organization in India, faced a difficult tax-compliance challenge that required responsible leadership and accountability from the whole team to overcome the challenge together.

Due to a significant oversight by Aanya's tax collection department, nobody had collected a required interstate tax form from clients. Out of compliance with Indian law, her organization was facing a threat of exposure to crores rupees (effectively millions of dollars) in sales tax payments. Recognizing that it had been her responsibility to make sure her team had been collecting those forms, Aanya knew she had to own the problem and make significant changes to fix the issue to mitigate the financial impact.

Accountability by the leader, in this example, exposes the complex process often needed to correct errors. In other words, being accountable is much more than accepting fault. Accountable leadership includes making right whatever may have been wrong.

Aanya started by gathering all the information she needed about the problem. She assembled the tax forms that had not yet been completed and assessed the potential financial loss that would occur if the forms remained undone. Immediately, she worked with her team to identify form submission deadlines expected by the Indian Revenue Service.

Modeling accountability, Aanya worked intensely with her team to correct the situation. Everybody, Anybody, Somebody, and Nobody, figuratively speaking, were excused from the room, and the whole team began to work feverishly together. Aanya united the team by painting a clear and accurate picture of the issue and empowered the team to participate in designing the process that would be needed to resolve the issue. They in turn became accountable and created urgency to meet the deadline imposed by the Indian Revenue Service.

First, they organized a project plan. Next, Aanya personally alerted her director about the issue and her culpability. Although he, of course, was not at all happy that the team had put the organization in this position, the director cooperated in resolving the error. Aanya committed to take full responsibility for the situation and showed the director the team's new plan. Consulting the director, she decided on setting the goal to collect at least 95 percent of the forms needed before the 3-month deadline. She also set an interim milestone goal to collect at least 50 percent of the forms from her top client list within the first 45 days.

Aanya also called a meeting with others in the organization to bring attention to the issue, present the plan to collect the forms, and assign tasks to responsible parties. Learning from the mistake, she also set up weekly accountability meetings with her management team to ensure project progress and completion in the future.

As planned and because of the responsible actions of Aanya and her team, they collected the missing forms worth over $1.4 million in tax liability!

Every leader can learn or relearn a lesson from this example. **Accountability starts with you.** Don't attempt to delegate accountability to deflect blame from yourself. Leaders with integrity will shoulder responsibility, fix the issues, and implement processes to prevent future mishaps. Although individuals on Aanya's team had neglected collecting the forms from clients, she had assumed responsibility as the department head once the issue surfaced. Those who may have caused the error were also included in developing and delivering the solution.

Decision Making

Driving the achievement of goals is also facilitated by well-thought-out decisions. When your decisions align with your values and your team is included in the decision-making process, achieving results becomes a shared set of goals.

Leaders make decisions daily, although some decisions are certainly larger than others. Leaders who make smart decisions in the open may at the same time be demonstrating to team members how to make good decisions themselves, especially in ways that may affect business opportunities in the future.

Do you consult others when you make decisions? Do you seek perspectives from your team? Or, do you decide alone? The way you approach a decision may depend on the nature of specific situations. Monetary decisions, organizational decisions, corrective decisions, and a variety of other resolutions might be handled very differently with each type of decision. Irrespective of the type of decision, ethical leaders are careful and intentional to not deceive, blame, or run afoul of promises made to others.

"When your values are clear to you, making decisions becomes easier." The quote, attributed to Roy Disney, nephew to Walt and longtime executive at the Walt Disney Company, links values to decision making. Leaders who drive for results find ways to link their organization's values with the major and minor decisions made every day.

When the values of your organization are understood and followed, making the right decisions and creating buy-in from your employees are typically easier. Whenever possible, everyone ought to know why the decision was made, not because of rules, regulations, policies, and procedures but because the decision is aligned with the values that guide them. Values answer the question of how you go about doing business. They answer how organizations should manufacture products, deliver services, market themselves, and treat customers—and also how managers treat employees.

Miguel, a senior manager in a medical products manufacturing organization in the Dominican Republic, was tasked to lead a major $25.5 million cost-reduction project at his manufacturing plant. Faced with significant cost-cutting demands, he decided to act collaboratively with those on his team. From past experience, he felt that a slash-and-burn approach to cutting costs was not effective or sustainable. Miguel determined to make decisions with high team engagement and involvement. The first decision he made was aligning the project plan with the values of the organization. He also understood that he needed a strong team of cross-functional leaders, leaders who could communicate the need for the changes and help guide the organization through completion of the plan.

In consideration of the talented people on his team, Miguel intended to retain employees and looked for ways to upgrade the skills and capabilities of his managers so that they might contribute in decisions that would affect the whole organization. In this instance, a leadership development course addressed a longer-term plan. Situations like Miguel's predicament may require immediate action, as well as decisions to grow the capacity or skills necessary to handle persistent challenges. The best solutions may require an investment of time and a growth-focused approach to meet organizational needs.

Miguel decided, with input from his managers, to enroll in leadership development training that would help his team unify and access month-to-month a much larger set of leadership tools. Showing commitment to the team's development goals, Miguel inserted the monthly leadership development program into the cost-savings project plan. The cost-savings directive led to leadership training, which resulted in the leadership team coming up with thoughtful solutions together. As a consequence of participating together, managers presented new ideas related to process improvements, employee morale and performance, and shifts in focus to cost-saving innovations. They also decided to hold one another accountable as they worked over the year to implement new ideas. Miguel and his team exceeded cost-reduction targets, achieving an annual cost savings of $30.3 million.

Miguel could have made the decision to take the short-term approach to cost reduction as managers may do, particularly in the manufacturing industry, by laying off employees and expecting more from less. Instead, he was able to keep his focus on the ultimate goal of improving business processes. He developed needed skills within his team and led his managers to collaborate on creating a sustainable cost-reduction initiative that ultimately allowed the organization to grow revenue and capacity. The actions of his team were aligned with the values of the organization. In effect, he **slowed down to speed up**, and it paid dividends that would enlarge the skills and capabilities far beyond the immediate project to cut costs.

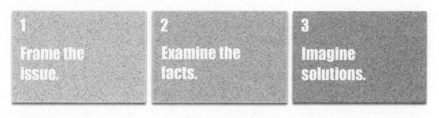

1 Frame the issue.	2 Examine the facts.	3 Imagine solutions.
Talk it out or think it out. Every decision should be based on a clear picture of the objective and the current situation. Where do you want to be? Where are you now?	Making good decisions means not making hasty decisions. Discover the facts, egos, perceptions, attitudes, outlooks, and history of the issue and the people involved.	Focus on more than one solution rather than jumping at the first and ask the right questions. What assumptions are we making? What if? Why not? What's the timeline?

Figure 1.1   Simple Decision-Making Process

Various decision-making models have been abundantly shared online, and some are more elaborate than others. At the instance you need to make a decision, knowing a simple and easy-to-recall model can help you consistently respond.

The essential first step in decision making is to frame the issue. Working with a team or alone, examine available information relating to the issue and list possible actions that might resolve the issue. Frame it. Examine relevant facts and perspectives. Imagine possible actions.

Decision-making leaders who focus on finding more than one solution, as opposed to jumping at the first solution that comes to mind, are apt to find in their ideas one that addresses the issue better than alternatives. Asking the right questions, therefore, is the way to imagine possible actions. Managers might overthink decisions using complex or academic models, although some decisions may require a more extensive process framework. In most cases, simplicity and clarity lead to sound decisions.

> When starting a new project, do you take the time to slow down to speed up?

Asking the Right Questions

Accountability and good decision making depend on asking the right questions. Leaders who know how to ask the right questions have a greater ability to collect the information and knowledge they need to make good decisions. Think about the questions you should be asking in terms of the *Afters* of the decision. **Afters describe the ultimate goal.**

A developer built a residential neighborhood and hired an architectural firm to design a swimming pool for placement at the entrance of the new community. "A big pool," he said when explaining the project to the architect. When the firm finished and presented a scale model of their big swimming pool design, the developer paused and then said, "That's not at all what I wanted." Dismayed, the architect who believed he had followed the builder's request for a big pool asked, "Then what DO you want?"

What happened next illustrates the concept and importance of Afters. The developer responded, "When a family drives by the new community, I want the children to feel excited by slides and attractions like you'd see at a water park and shout 'Mom and Dad, I want to live there!'"

Had the developer started with the Afters before the architect invested time and resources into building a scale model of a large swimming pool, he would have effectively communicated his vision of what has to be achieved as a result of constructing the pool area: "Mom and Dad, I want to live there!" That is the Afters effect, and the Afters effect should always be stated at the beginning of a project, not the end.

The best way to get exactly what you want, the first time, is to find the Afters by asking future-based questions that focus on results and deliverables. **Ask yourself: "What am I looking to achieve?" and "What must happen after this project is done for this to be successful?"**

Next, dig deeper with second-line questions. People are motivated by their wants, but they also need to define what their companies need. Second-line questions reveal the who, what, where, and when of a project or initiative and fill in the blanks to get the whole picture. Subtle phrases such as, "Tell me more," or "Say more about that" are useful prompts when trying to understand someone else's request. Second-line questions also help to draw out additional information, such as how to prioritize multiple goals or results.

Finally, when tasked by someone else, after you have asked second-line questions for clarity, ask one more: "Anything else?" and then listen.

Once the desired results and priorities are determined, repeat the details back to make sure you understood. Give clear options for how the work and results can be achieved and let stakeholders choose their own path to completion.

Future-based questions can clarify the Afters when asked, and that generally makes communication more productive. Future-based questions you might ask to others or to you yourself include:

• What would you love your team to have that they do not have now?

- Where do you want to be in 1, 3, 5, or 10 years?
- What are you looking to achieve from this?

The answers to those questions are the Afters, and they do not always come easily. **The Afters must be specific and focused on the future.** They set a clear vision of what the end result of the project will mean for the organization, so do not stop with the first question. Remember that it is a descriptive picture of the future that you are trying to discover. Merely asking one or two questions is not as helpful, unless those questions help to pinpoint the ultimate success. What has to happen in the future as a result of this project? If this project is going to succeed, what will that look like in the future? Asking future-based questions helps teams drive for results by solidifying the vision and clarifying what the results mean to the organization.

> Are you asking probing questions to understand future needs?

Imagine that you are assigned to write a report and you ask, "What are you looking to achieve from this report?" The answer to that question and subsequent questions can give you very clear direction on the impact that will later be expected once the report has been completed. It would be a mistake to go, "Great, I'll just go and write your report then!" Without asking the right questions first, you will not have gotten the clarity you need. Second- and third-line questions may also be helpful. Asking the right questions can prevent frustrating rework that occurs when *doing* first replaces *questioning* first.

A series of good questions can also assist managers in communicating more productively with their employees. Consider a single example of asking second, third, fourth, and even fifth questions to genuinely understand work-related situations and engage an employee as you make decisions.

Additional questions can become second nature to leaders who practice asking follow-up questions. For example, imagine an employee has complained about his involvement on a project team. The manager has asked, "How's the project team doing?"

"It's not working," the employee responds.

The manager then asks a second question, "Oh really? Why do you say that?" You might observe that the employee's response lacked clarity.

After the manager has asked the follow-up questions, the employee is quick to answer, "Well I'm just not enjoying it very much."

The third question in this example illustrates the value of asking the right questions. The right question here was probing. The manager asked, "When did this start? Is this a recent thing?"

Develop a list of probing questions that could uncover root causes or bring clarity to comments made by others. After asking, "When did this start," the manager might have also asked, "What do you think is causing this?"

If the discussion, in this scenario, has led to a resolution or change, asking another follow-up question can transform the outlook of the employee. The manager asks, "How do you think this change can help you enjoy it more?" and so on.

If you ask more second-line questions, you get more complete information. "Anything else?" is then a perfect question to ask after you have finished asking a series of discovery questions. This additional question can unlock ideas or concerns you have not yet considered.

This is an exercise you can do alone by asking yourself these questions privately to help drill down to the root issues or underlying need prior to tasking others with a project or assignment. As a result, your communication can be much clearer, and the Afters much more easily defined and expressed. **Asking the right questions with your team also ensures that everyone is fully aware of what you want to achieve with a new project or initiative.**

The concept of Afters not only directs you in asking the right questions to collect the information you need to make better decisions, it also helps increase employee productivity and morale. Teach Afters and future-based questions to your team and be open to the members of your team asking you these questions as you are assigning them new projects. When everyone on the team is Afters-oriented, communication and deliverables are far more efficient and productive because you and your team communicate with impact and deliver what is truly important—the first time.

A leader who is effective at driving for results is keenly focused on what is most important to achieving the strategic goals of the organization and is able to create a balanced sense of urgency around those tactics that contribute to the strategic direction. The leader makes decisions based on the ability of his or her associates to identify and fully understand the business need—or what has to happen after the project is complete for the project to be considered a success. The leader then takes action consistent with the available facts and information.

Driving for results sometimes requires quick action. At other times, it is part of a long-term, strategic vision. The results-driven leader plans, measures, tracks, revisits, and holds people accountable. Irrespective of whether an initiative takes days, weeks, months, or years, leaders who formulate and execute plans to drive for results succeed in improving the performance of their teams and the value of their organizations.

Core Competency: Drives for Results

Focuses on what is important and creates a sense of urgency, successfully managing multiple priorities. Implements tracking and follow-up mechanisms to ensure rapid progress. Identifies and understands issues and takes action that is consistent with available facts and risk.

Competency Skills
- **Accountability:** Establishes clear responsibilities and processes for monitoring, communicating progress, and measuring results
- **Decision Making:** Uses the information available and best judgment to make a timely decision
- **Asking the Right Questions:** Probes the thought process of others and asks the right questions to uncover root causes to problems and better solutions

Drives for Results Assessment Questions

1. Do your employees own the results of the projects and initiatives assigned to them? Do they own and drive for results, or do they merely go through the motion of effort?
2. What is your tracking mechanism for your department's goals?
3. How do you ensure accountability? Start by answering these questions. Do all projects and initiatives have:
   a. A goal—what does winning look like?
   b. One clear owner?
   c. A project plan with dates, deliverables, and a point person for each deliverable?
   d. A standard check-in process for deliverables?
4. When starting a new project, do you take the time to slow down to speed up?
5. Are you asking probing questions to understand future needs?

The Leader's Toolkit

1. Are you accountable to organizational values when you decide on actions that affect others?
   a. List the stated values of your organization.

   b. Describe in writing how each value should influence decisions made on your team or by you or someone in your organization.

The Afters of this simple exercise are to always drive decisions based on holding yourself accountable to the values you claim as an organization.

2. Are you asking the right questions? Create a list of five future-based questions that you could ask yourself or others to ensure an accurate understanding of the underlying purpose of any project.

Builds the Right Team

E very year since 1973, mushers and dogs have competed in a race once
reported by British journalist Ian Woolridge as "the only really great race
left." The Iditarod, a sled dog race through the unforgiving Alaskan
wilderness, is a story of teams.

The winning team is the first to travel from Anchorage to Nome, through
storms and bitter temperatures below negative 45 degrees Celsius. With 1,770
kilometers (1,100 miles) of rough terrain and deep, often treacherous, snow and
40-knot headwind, reaching the finish line is 10 to 20 full days away from when
the race begins.

Although it may be unusual to compare a team of 16 dogs to a team of people,
the champion leader in both situations always assembles the right talent, organizes
and develops specific and intentional roles, and manages diversity and differences.

One of those champions is Libby Riddles. On the 20th of March 1985, 18 days,
20 minutes, and 17 seconds after leaving Anchorage, she became the first woman
in history to win the Iditarod and proved the value of building a great team.
Mushing with a team of home-bred and trained sled dogs, Riddles made a pivotal
decision at the checkpoint in Shaktoolik before the sun rose on the fifteenth day.
While her competitors waited out a harrowing blizzard, she drove her team into
the 40-knot headwind, zipping herself into her sled bag and spending a night
camping alone with her dogs in the snow when visibility vanished. Libby knew
that her decision to drive into the storm was a move that would be tough on her
dogs, particularly the leaders of the pack, but her dedication to caring for, training,
and building a relationship of mutual trust with her dogs made this bold move
the thing that separated her from the competition and enabled her to clinch the
victory.

Riddles is the first to credit her 16 dogs, handpicked and trained from her personal kennel of 50, as the reason for her success. In an interview with Sled Dog Central, she described her well-synchronized team and the unique contributions of each dog. Seeing herself as the coach and having a keen awareness of the different physical abilities and emotional and mental skills of each member of her team, she figured out how to make each dog reach its potential.

Not every manager can drive a team into a blizzard, not without severe costs. But a strong leader can achieve amazing feats if he or she first builds the right team. Champion leaders cultivate the ability to build, organize, develop, and unify.

The goal of a great leader and manager is to create a champion team in which every team member knows, understands, and is committed to the organization's success. Building and maintaining such a team is not easy; it takes preparation and commitment. You must make sure that you begin with having the right people on your team through an effective hiring process. Then, you must be able to retain those employees and keep them engaged, focused, committed, and motivated through validation and development.

Hiring the Right Talent

Building a champion team starts with attracting and hiring the right team members. A Gallup study found that companies fail to choose the job candidate with the right talent for the position 82 percent of the time.[1] Yet, this is perhaps the most important decision that leaders need to make. To be successful in today's fast-paced, customer-centric business environment, companies must have the right employees who love what they do.

A wise leader will pursue candidates who come from different backgrounds and have diverse styles, perspectives, and strengths, while also having a personality that will integrate well with the culture of the organization.

Of course, your candidate needs to have the technical skills and experience to be able to perform the duties assigned to the role with excellence. These are aspects that often can be assessed from résumés and references. But how does a manager make an educated decision about the candidate's drive or ability to think critically and solve problems strategically? How can a manager assess the candidate's level of emotional intelligence and ability to work well with the rest of the team? The interview plays a critical role in answering these questions and making the best determination if the candidate is the right fit; however, the interview process is only as effective as the questions that are asked and the process used.

Linda, the general manager of a quickly growing orthopedic practice in the United States, needed to hire two new physician assistant positions. She had hired, trained, managed, and fired employees in the past, but she never had a formal process for doing so. She always tried her best to make the right decision, yet she relied on résumés to identify the person she hoped would have the right background, experience, and skills to fill the position. She searched the Internet for information on conducting interviews and found lists of questions to ask. But sometimes it just seemed as though she had to go with her instincts and then hope for the best. Like many managers often do, she made her decision on the fit of a candidate before seeing the candidate in action.

But this time around, Linda had a new hiring and interviewing process that she had learned by participating in a leadership development program, and she was looking forward to trying her improved hiring methods with the next applicant. First, she took the time to think about and write down the key competencies of all the physician assistants already on the team who were exceptional employees. They were committed to their work, were friendly with the clients and the rest of the team, could do exceptional work under pressure, and had the technical competence and drive to proactively identify and act on physicians' and clients' needs. Using this as her baseline, she developed a job description that outlined these important key competencies of a qualified candidate. She also used them to draft related interview questions that she and her interview panel would use when they found candidates to interview.

Résumés emphasize technical skills, but they give little insight into soft skills such as emotional intelligence, communication, commitment, and proactive behavior. Linda knew that she needed to **align her behavior-based questions with the key competencies needed to make the new hires successful.**

Linda selected a pool of 10 applicants to conduct an initial phone interview. This initial interview was to get a quick assessment of the candidates' phone communication skills—how do they answer their own phone? How well do they speak and present themselves over the phone? She also used this time to review their résumés with them and to ask clarifying questions about their backgrounds and technical skills. For example, she said, "You indicated your technical skills include the Allscripts Electronic Medical Records system that we use. How comfortable are you with using this system? How long have you been using it?"

Based on the 10 phone interviews that she conducted, Linda categorized them from strongest to weakest and then chose the top seven candidates to invite to an in-person interview. This is when she included two additional colleagues to make up her interview panel; they focused on behavior-based questions.

Linda took part in the in-person interviews, along with one of their excellent physician assistants and a physician. She split her list of questions into three sections and sent them to each person on the interview panel, along with the seven résumés. She also invited the other two panel interviewers to include questions of their own that would be considered important to them in their specific roles. Sitting together, each panel member asked questions. These included questions that required the applicants to answer by sharing relevant experiences.

The answers to behavior questions provide information, but more importantly they give clues to the level of soft skills and whether a candidate possesses the key competencies needed to be successful. For example, Linda would ask, "Tell me about a time when you had to work with a client who was consistently not following their therapy schedule." After hearing the response, and based on the information shared by a particular candidate, she asked two follow-up behavioral questions: "How did you convince them to do what they needed to do?" and "What were the results?"

The process continued with additional sharing from the applicant, followed by behavior-based questions. "Tell me about a time when you worked with a physician who you thought was difficult to work with." Then, "What made you feel as though he or she was difficult to work with?" and "How did you resolve this issue?"

After each interview, the interview panel briefly discussed their assessment of each candidate and rated them on a scale from 1 to 7 (the number of candidates they were interviewing). This interview process led Linda to extend an offer of employment to two candidates who the three interviewers agreed would be best-suited for the job.

Behavior-based questions are a key component of the interviewing process that help you identify if the candidate has the soft skills required to perform the job well. These questions do not waste time with hypothetical inquiries. Rather, they help you understand in detail how candidates acted in specific situations. Many behavioral questions begin with "Tell me about a time when . . ." or "Tell me about. . . ." When you ask the candidate to talk about a specific type of experience make sure to align the rest of the questions around the key competencies you are hiring for. Some examples of commonly used behavioral questions include:

- Tell me about a goal you set that you did not reach. What steps did you take? What obstacles did you encounter?
- Give an example of how you handled a difficult situation with a customer.
- Tell me about something new or different you initiated that improved productivity. What was the impact and how did you measure it?
- Tell me about one of the toughest groups you have had to work with. What made it difficult? What did you do?
- Give me an example of a time you had to adjust quickly to changes over which you had no control. What was the impact of the change on you?

Using an interviewing panel rather than one-on-one interviews eliminates the tendency for candidates to be asked the same question multiple times.

Interviewing panels also allow the interviewers the advantage of hearing and seeing the candidate's responses to others' questions. Each candidate should be asked the same questions by the same interviewing panel member. Each interviewer on the panel can be assigned a specific selection of questions to ask while the others observe and take notes. You may decide to split up the questions based on how the candidate will be interacting with the other members of the interviewing panel, or you might break them into more functional sections, such as leadership key competencies, values, and technical skills specific to the job.

An Interview Competency Evaluation Form helps facilitate and organize the interview-by-panel process. At the end of the interview, the panelists complete their evaluation form and report on their feedback during a debrief meeting facilitated by the hiring manager or human resources manager.

About a month after hiring the two new physician assistants, one of the doctors complemented Linda's hiring decision during the monthly doctors meeting.

"These two new assistants you hired are great, Linda!" she exclaimed. "Where did you find them?"

"It's not *where* I found them," Linda replied. "It's *how* I found them."

At their insistence, she briefly explained her new interviewing process to the doctors. "I wish we had this a long time ago," said another doctor. "If we had been asking these kinds of questions earlier, we would have saved ourselves a lot of mistakes—and money!"

> What is your process for selecting the right talent for your team?

Interviewing is a key component to building the right team in your organization, but it is only the beginning. Once you have found the right candidate, onboarding is the next component that lays the groundwork for the entire employee-employer relationship dynamic. **Onboarding produces higher employee engagement, retention, and an understanding of roles within the organization.** It also infuses your workers with your organization's culture, the "why we do what we do," and builds the groundwork for why employees should care. A great onboarding process includes four components: prelaunch, administrative, organizational, and technical.

The prelaunch component needs to happen before the new hire's first day. This includes ensuring that the new hire's computer, desk, telephone, and passwords are in place or created. Perhaps business cards should be ordered. New supervisors and employees may also need access to tools, vehicles, or training. These types of needs should be addressed before the arrival of the new employee. Also, be sure to let other team members know when the new hire will be arriving.

The administrative component of onboarding takes care of all the paperwork that needs to be filled out, signed, and submitted by the new employee. These first two components of onboarding may seem mundane, but they are important steps to be made. They ensure that the new employee is able to begin focusing on training and the important elements of the job as quickly as possible. They also provide a great first impression on the new employee and help him or her feel valued.

The organizational component of your onboarding process focuses on making sure that your organization's vision, mission, values, and strategy are clearly communicated. Show the new employee your organization chart and explain how your organization is structured and identify the key people in the organization. Then do a walk-through to introduce team members to the new member. The hiring manager should also **send an organization-wide email welcoming the new hire to help them feel welcomed in the new position.** The organizational component of your onboarding process is critical to getting new employees oriented with the overall culture and direction of your organization.

The fourth component of a great onboarding process is the technical component. This covers the specifics of the new employee's position, duties, and goals. In the technical part of your onboarding process, include communicating the manager's expectations, department goals, and who to approach with questions, as well as the team's preferred communication mechanism—such as email, meeting, text, intraweb, and messenger. It should also **outline the specific expectations for the first 30 days and set up performance goals for the rest of the year.** In addition, the technical component should provide an overview of general business processes and systems, such as expense reporting, vacation requests, phones, and shared networks.

What is your process for onboarding talent? Do your team members understand your expectations and how to thrive as a member of your team?

Your goal in hiring the right talent is finding team members who are competent, committed, and collaborative contributors. Hiring the right talent is just the first step to building the right team. Using these hiring and onboarding tactics will help get your new hire off on the right foot, but retaining employees and developing them into a winning team requires organization and development.

Multigenerational Leadership

Building a team that will go with you into the blizzard requires harnessing the potential provided by employees, associates, or peers whose ages range from 18 to

70 years. Developing a champion team that can communicate, collaborate, and coordinate effectively is complicated by the diversity of generations that exist in the average workplace. However, leaders who understand and engage generational expectations, perspectives, and opportunities will distance their teams ahead of competitors.

The workforce has entered a phase like we have never been in before. We used to have two generations, maybe three, in the workplace. **Now, you are managing sometimes four generations, even five, on the same team.** No matter where you are in the world, what industry you are in, or what kind of organization you are in, you are part of the biggest demographic shift the workplace has ever seen.

Baby Boomers are living and working longer than those in past generations, while at the same time, Generation Yers have entered the workplace in such numbers that they outnumber both the Boomers and the Gen X employees. Technology has changed so quickly in recent decades that each of these generations generally works and communicates very differently from each other. Gen Zers, those generally born between 1996 and 2015, are now just being introduced to the workforce. Managing this multigenerational workforce introduces a new and unique set of challenges, and you will need the ability to motivate, engage, and communicate with each of these generations. Perhaps most importantly, you must be able to draw on each of their strengths.

Because generational groups around the world experience many of the same formative experiences, especially in terms of economic, parenting, and educational trends, they come into the workplace with very similar expectations, a similar outlook, and with similar ways of getting work done. No matter what their expectations or work habits are, **each generation has their own set of strengths that make them an important, relevant part of your team.**

Baby Boomers have generally been employed for a longer span of time than more recent generations, and they are potentially some of the most passionate and optimistic people on your team, traits that you cannot train or easily develop. When Boomers were growing up, there was more time, and the pace of change—especially technological change—typically was much slower. Boomers likely grew up reasoning that things take time. They may have learned to get work done by using interpersonal, face-to-face relationships. You may notice that Boomers really are more comfortable in meetings because that is how they know, or prefer, to get things done.

Generation X is the group next in age. Gen Xers have qualities that you may appreciate as a leader. Gen Xers tend to be independent, efficient, and likely to ask the hard questions. When Gen Xers were children and teens, globalization was an emerging economic concept. Old economies were being disrupted, and traditionally stable industries began to fail. There was more competition and more complexity in the economy. Gen Xers witnessed a lot of traditional jobs being

CRESTCOM

	Generation B "Boomers" 1945 - 1960	Generation X "Gen X" 1961 - 1980	Generation Y "Millennials" or "Gen Y" 1981 - 1995	Generation Z "Gen Z" or "iGen" 1996 - 2015
Personality	Optimistic Cause-Oriented Collaborative Driven	Independent Self-Reliant Skeptical	Continuously Learning High Self-Esteem Achievement-Oriented	Resilient Technology-Savvy Less Entitled
Work Ethic	Quality Minded Team-Oriented Company Loyalty	Work-Life Balance Efficient Focus on Results	Collaborative Desires Feedback Flexible Work Arrangements	Resourceful Meaningful Work Strong Work Ethic
Communication	Rotary Dial Telephone Face-to-Face	Email Text	Instant Message Text	Text Social Media
Technology	Touch-tone Telephone TV Calculator	Touch-tone Telephone Pager Word Processor	Desktops Cell Phones Internet	Tablets Smartphones Social Media

Register online for additional resources: crestcomleadership.com | 1-888-CRESTCOM.

Figure 2.1 Generational Personalities, Work Ethics, Communication Channels, and Technology.

lost and new expectations being established for workers as the world changed. Technological changes and global shifts appear to have made Gen Xers more prone to skepticism and self-reliance. A common stereotype is that people in Gen X prefer to work by themselves and avoid meetings, especially the myriad meetings organized by the Boomers.

Generation Yers, also known as Millennials, were socialized differently than either of the two previous generations. Maybe this is attributable to growing pressures from more scarcity and less abundance. The expectations of past generations regarding education, entry into the workforce, and ability to provide for oneself were confronted by newer realities worldwide. Culture shifted from just skepticism to urgency. Gen Y employees tend to collaborate better than those from Gen X. They grew up online, and they have lived in a culture of constant give and take. They could create content online, or they could consume others' content, concepts unfamiliar to most Boomers. They also have generally expected to be asked for input in making decisions about things that could affect their work. In fact, Gen Y employees may insist on being consulted because they generally work best when they work collaboratively.

Gen Y has been criticized for not being loyal to employers, and it is true that they will make more job changes throughout their careers than either of the prior generations of workers. That said, much of their loyalty depends on your ability as a leader to give them the chance to have input, to structure ways in which they are always able to ask questions and work collaboratively. In the right environment, Gen Y employees can be highly efficient workers, getting work accomplished urgently. They are comfortable using technology to increase productivity, and they can shift with changes and innovations relatively quickly because of the rapid pace of changes experienced throughout their lives. Generating ideas and coming up with new ways to do things can be valuable to you as a leader.

Now emerging in the workforce, Gen Z is very different from the Gen Y because the mood of the world appears to have shifted from urgent to practical during their formative years. They are accustomed to worrying about whether there will be a job for them when they get out of school. They may expect to have to work hard to be successful. If Gen Z does not have a solution, they will find a solution. If they cannot find a solution, they will make one. We might begin to predict the impact of Gen Z on the teams you lead, but time will tell.

Whereas managers tend to focus on the differences between the generations, ones who build champion teams know how to harness the strengths of the different generations present on the team. One of the ways they can do this is through mentoring. Although people often think about mentoring in terms of more experienced individuals mentoring younger employees, the fact is that nearly everyone has something that can be shared to help improve the skills of others. For this reason, **fostering collaborative, multigenerational mentoring relationships is important for the development of your champion team.**

Jerry, the director of operations in an international health services organization based in the United States, managed a team of well-qualified employees. The team reevaluated global trends and the competition in their industry before beginning a realignment of the organization's services with new market expectations and opportunities. As they converted many operational processes to more technology-driven tools, Jerry discovered for himself an opportunity to learn new skills. In fact, the most qualified teacher was the youngest member of his team.

Wanting a more thorough understanding of the cloud-based tools adopted by the organization to handle internal and corporate communications, Jerry engaged his team member in a mentoring relationship wholly based on her skills and not on her age or experience in the organization. Mentoring works in both directions in a collaborative multigenerational workforce through mentoring programs where employees mentor each other without regard for age, but instead skills and experience. For example, more experienced employees mentor younger employees on topics such as executive presence and fostering relationships, while younger employees mentor others on using technology and collaborative innovation.

How to attract and retain new employees who may not share similar expectations or behavioral norms shows up commonly in leadership development trainings because of the criticality of organizing and developing contemporary teams that function well together. Engaging and collaborating with team members in different generations, as Jerry did, is what multigenerational leadership is about. Becoming a multigenerational leader requires recalibrating your assumptions and adapting your organization to focus on shared values, regardless of age.

Clearly, each generation on your team has their differences but also some shared values and interests. They each have different ways of working and communicating. **The best way to manage a multigenerational team and engage them to perform better is to focus on the values that they share and the ways in which the strengths of one can balance the opportunities in others.** There are many values that all the generations on your team share. One, for example, is *respect*. No matter what generation you are dealing with, it is important for that person to feel respected at work; however, this value plays out in completely different ways for different generations. Gen Yers feel respected when you listen to their input and when you structure a way to make sure that they have a voice in decisions. Gen Xers feels respected when you leave them alone and do not micromanage. That is because Xers can be very covetous of their time. For Xers, time is the most valuable resource; when you respect their time, you respect them. Thus, when you excuse them from meetings and do not block their work with bureaucracy, they tend to be happier. For Boomers, respect is best conveyed when people talk to them, look at them, and show with body language and a voice that honors their opinions and acknowledges their experience.

Another value that all generations share is the value of **loyalty**. Traditionally, loyalty has meant staying with the same organization, perhaps throughout your whole career. But in recent decades, that kind of agreement between employer and employee was broken, and job stability became a thing of the past in most markets around the world. What does loyalty mean now? Employees have begun to shift from loyalty to an organization to loyalty for other things, such as to quality of life, to an immediate supervisor as opposed to an organization, or to learning new career-enhancing skills rather than learning how to move up in one organization. By understanding what your employees are loyal to, you can enhance the loyalty of your employees on a more individual basis. Your younger employees may be looking to develop their technical skills while they are building their careers and their portfolios, but your older Gen Yers and Gen Xers may be more interested in higher-level education such as leadership development and executive coaching. Boomers generally are more loyal to the organization naturally because that is how they developed in the earlier years of their careers.

All generations value *community*. Everyone wants to work with people they enjoy working with and who appreciate each other. When you create opportunities for positive association, you are likely to find all generations find that rewarding. Simple appreciation for events such as birthdays or celebrations are absolutely considered rewards by all the generations—as long as they do not take up too much time.

Work ethic is a common value that tends to be a hot-button issue between generations. Work ethic means something a little different to each generation because each is shaped by the period when they entered the workforce. Boomers consider part of work ethic to be on time, in your seat, face to face. But, for Xers, good work ethic is about results, not a physical presence. It is Gen X that began including work–life balance in the work ethic. Gen Xers believes in the importance of balance, that they are better workers if they have time for family, friends, and life. It keeps them from burning out. Gen Y takes work–life balance one step further. They expect work–life integration. Gen Y expects to be able to take time off during the day to do personal things, but then they will go home and work until late at night getting the work done. Gen Z is just coming along, and we know they are going to work hard, but we really have yet to discover what exactly their work ethic looks like. They tend to be very close to their families, so work–life balance is likely to be an expectation for Gen Z employees.

Generational *communication* is an issue that mystifies leaders. Generally, it is true that Gen Y and Z have preferred text communication—quick bits and bytes of information. Gen X as a group prefers email, whereas Boomers prefer phone calls or face-to-face communication. However, you cannot assume this true for every-body. Communication preferences are very individualistic. Ultimately, **the best way to find out how each person on your team prefers to communicate is to simply ask.** Also, ask the important question of what motivates them.

> How are you leveraging the strengths of all the generations in your organization?

Building the right team is not a one-time event, it includes hiring, organizing, and developing a champion team that is committed to working together to achieve the organization's vision. The champion team can execute the organiza-tion's strategy through values-based coordination, communication, and collabo-ration. A champion team does not consist of one type of person; rather, a great leader will be able to recruit a diversity of strengths, knowledge, and experiences and leverage those differences to create a strategic strength for the organization.

Organizing and Developing Teams

Building champion teams that excel together requires ongoing development and leadership. Great teams are aligned on team goals and how those goals tie into the organization's vision, mission, and strategy. Everyone on a great team understands how he or she adds value to the team and works to help others on the team succeed. Team members understand if the team succeeds, they succeed.

Champion teams are developed when team members can communicate openly and share ideas. They are also able to give and receive feedback both laterally and vertically. They are more concerned about the usefulness of the feedback than the source. Common goals and open communication feed a culture of cooperation and productivity. **Champion team members can connect individual performance to team success and team success to organization vision.** This is achieved by involving the team members in the development of the team goals. Once the team goals are established, it is key to ensure that every team member commits to the goals. Lastly, each team member must define and share how he or she will contribute to reaching these goals.

A remarkable example of team development occurred within a software organization in a competitive software-services market in the United States. Recently appointed as the new product development director, Steve's new job involved creating a new team. Most of the members of the new team would come from within the organization because Steve studied the staff to select talented developers and engineers. Two of the members of the team would come from outside recruitment.

After interviews, Steve decided to hire two developers who had been highly recommended by a top regional school. Steve surmised that the new team would benefit from fresh perspectives, especially from talented graduates who had excelled in their recent training.

Once assembled, the individuals on the team struggled to work well together. The first few team meetings revealed tension between the developers who had been with the company before and the two newly hired employees. Inflated egos contributed to the tension, especially when the more experienced developers were rubbed the wrong way because they believed the recent graduates had excessively high opinions of themselves.

For any manager working to build a cohesive and productive team, situations such as Steve's may require additional skills. His tangible experience in a leadership development course enabled Steve to weigh the best options for resolving personality-driven conflicts. By creating with the team a clear and unifying goals and matching responsibilities with strengths, Steve aligned the team around the development of a prototype with a very short deadline. The urgency required to complete the prototype on time focused the team on working together, at least initially.

Despite applying learned techniques for teambuilding, Steve discovered that, however important, a motivating goal alone was insufficient to build cooperation and soften the egos that made the process difficult. The team missed the deadline and settled on a prototype after three attempts. As team members continued to focus chiefly on themselves rather than engaging more as a team, the deadline became a source of frustration rather than unity. The overtime hours needed to get the prototype ready for senior staff approval further triggered conflict within the team.

Steve was convinced of the potential to transform his talented engineers and developers into a cohesive team and began to implement steps to move them to be more efficient working together. **Poor performance by one or a few individuals can be detrimental, but the effect of talented individuals working individually rather than as a team can produce the same negative energy and obstruct the hidden potential that could occur by the team working together.** In Steve's case, the members of his team generally performed well but not together. They were individual performers, not team players.

To organize the talented developers to work as a team, additional leadership intervention would be necessary, especially in opening dialogue that could address concerns directly. Steve communicated with team members to inspire a more collaborative approach. He got the team together to discuss what had occurred leading up to the missed deadline and what needed to change. He met with all team members separately to better understand what motivated them and how best to lead them. The one-on-one conversations allowed Steve to relate personally to the members and align how they saw their roles on the team and how they believed they could best contribute. He individually discussed with the two new recruits the importance of being part of a team and how they could leverage their talents and help the team be successful.

Developing your team members is as important to your organization's success as it is to the individual's success. Development happens in many ways that challenge people to venture outside their comfort zones to learn something new or do things that may require adapting to group dynamics. Effective leaders adopt a longer-term approach to developing the individuals on the team to ensure team cohesion. One-on-one time grooming individuals can also prime the organization with a pipeline of management or leadership-ready people who can step in and fill gaps as the organization grows.

Leaders plan and actively engage in building champion teams and grooming new leaders through mentoring. Mentoring also works to bind teams together by allowing team members to share in each other's strengths and experiences as they grow and improve.

During their next team meeting, Steve's team developed a **team charter that defined its purpose and how the members would work together as a team.** The charter was a simple document created together with guidelines that every member of the team agreed to follow. They discussed their goals for the year and how they would achieve these goals as a team. They discussed how they would handle conflict and provide one another feedback. The following day, each team member was tasked to set or revise individual goals to correspond to the team's plan, and they each presented to the team how they would cooperate to achieve the team's success.

Steve demonstrated the patience and skills to organize and develop a unified team. Despite the stormy beginning, the team developed cooperative rhythms and supportive habits that produced excellence consistently.

Developing a champion team starts with being an adaptive leader who builds bridges and inserts employees into positions that best match their strengths. Like the example, leaders must facilitate communication and help individual members align. If you do this in a way that focuses on shared values and encourages mutually beneficial interactions, you can turn individuals into a unified, productive team.

How are you recognizing your team's success? Is everyone proud to be a member of your team?

Core Competency: Builds the Right Team

Attracts, selects, and forms teams with diverse styles and perspectives. Fosters productive and collaborative teamwork and a sense of belonging for team members.

Competency Skills
- **Hiring the Right Talent:** Attracts and selects high-caliber talent to best meet the needs of the organization
- **Multigenerational Leadership:** Understands and values the importance of a generationally diverse workforce with different perspectives and working styles
- **Organizing and Developing Teams:** Establishes common goals and creates a collaborate sense of belonging team environment

---

Builds the Right Team Assessment Questions

1. What is your process for selecting the right talent for your team?
2. What is your process for onboarding talent? Do your team members understand your expectations and how to thrive as a member of your team?
3. How are you leveraging the strengths of all the generations in your organization?
4. How are you recognizing your team's success? Is everyone proud to be a member of your team?

The Leader's Toolkit

1. For your next open position, create a What Great Looks Like description. Think about the person who excels or has excelled in this role; this makes it real. Why is the person great? What are his or her strengths and experiences? Prioritize the behavior competencies given this profile. From this description, develop your job requirements and your interview questions. Ensure that your interview questions are aligned with the behavior competencies and are worded in an action-oriented/results format. For example, assume Results Orientation is a key behavior competency

required for this position. Here are a few questions you may want to consider in your interview process:

a. Tell us about the process that you have used to establish goals for your area. What were the process and steps you took? Were you satisfied with the outcome? Why or why not? What were your goals last year?

b. Tell us about a goal that you set that you did not reach. What obstacles did you encounter?

2. Hold a team retreat and define a team charter. This charter would include:

a. Purpose: What is the purpose of this team? How does this team add value to the organization?

b. Communication: How often does the team meet? Channel of communication?

c. Conflict Resolution: How does the team resolve conflicts?

d. Quality: How does the team measure quality?

Ensure that the team members get to know each other and understand each other's working style and strengths. Develop a team identity, celebrate wins, and solve issues together. Ensure that everyone on the team has a voice and feels valued.

CHAPTER

3

Influences Others

I n the context of business, a buzz can mean quiet chatter around the office. However, what if the buzz you hear in the office is not the employees talking but an actual colony of honeybees?

For an entrepreneur in Idaho, honey dripping from the ceiling was the clue that he was sharing his office space with a colony of bees. Although bees and people rarely share their workspace, we do share one common, specific social behavior—communicating.

Honeybees talk by dancing. Researchers have called this honeybee tango *the waggle dance*. What differentiates the waggle dance from interoffice and cross-departmental communication is the fact that it works perfectly nearly every time. For the bees, communication is instinctive, unlike humans who need training from infancy to learn how to communicate, and even more training as they advance in their careers to learn how to do it better.

Communication is a two-way process that affects every action, every project, and every outcome. Leaders who understand the impact and complexity are more likely to effectively influence outcomes, at least compared with those who may be indifferent to bettering their communication skills. Influence is the leader's most powerful tool because very little moves forward without it.

Organizational goals are achieved by leaders with the ability to influence and persuade others to do something, believe something, feel something, or learn something necessary for completing objectives. Through their level of ability to influence others, leaders either hold an organization together and propel it forward or they do not. Reflect on your own leadership experiences and consider how the ability to influence decisions, processes, relationships, and the quality and effectiveness of communication has contributed directly or indirectly to successes or failures in your organization.

The skills to effectively persuade or influence others are combined in a honeycomb of three distinct abilities. If you want to be more influential as a leader, work on (1) developing your skills in open and effective communication, (2) negotiation and building consensus, and (3) emotional intelligence. **Influence is how great leaders lead.**

Open and Effective Communication

As the honeybee's waggle dance illustrates, communication includes much more than simply talking. Communication includes body language, listening, asking, and sharing—in a word, *dialogue*. The ability to influence depends on effective communication. Although many leaders tout their communication skills, executives and managers often still default to a dictatorial approach rather than a persuasive one. Some managers believe a dictatorial approach is a more efficient way to communicate. This is a method of informing, not communicating.

Effective communication is less about talking and more about listening and fostering open, interested dialogue through asking the right questions, sharing information, participating in dialogue, and building consensus. **Leaders must become increasingly better at their inquiry skills versus their telling skills.** Great inquiry skills help employees obtain clarity, courage, and ownership of *their* recommendations.

Improve inquiry skills by:
- Maintaining a respectful and charge-neutral tone
- Asking open-ended questions
- Being genuinely inquisitive
- Making it safe by not interrogating
- Asking others to be specific

Examples of good inquiry questions:
- What do you want to have happen?
- What have you tried already?
- What is the most important thing to do now?
- How can I help?

During your one-on-one sessions with your employees, do you often talk more than listen?

Hannah, the director of accounts at an international process controls solutions organization based in the South Pacific, used a popular leadership tool to help facilitate open and effective communication with her team to improve the organization's customer experience metrics. Called the ⅓ + 1 Method, leaders around the world use this powerful tool to cultivate greater communication, encourage employee engagement, and build consensus among teams.

Step 1: Green Light Thinking

The ⅓ + 1 Method starts with an exercise called Green Light Thinking. In this exercise, give your team the opportunity to take 2 to 5 minutes to sit quietly and write what they think are your organization's or department's Coffee Stains.

Coffee Stains are those things about your organization that create an unpleasant customer experience. Often referring to the small things that make customers wonder if there are larger issues with quality control and operations.

It is important that you let everyone write down his or her own ideas privately. If you were to do it all at once as a group, some people will speak up with their ideas and others will not feel as comfortable speaking out in front of the group for a number of reasons. You want the ideas and perspectives of everyone in the group to create consensus, as well as to gain each person's unique perspective on an issue, because he or she has to deal with it in the context of his or her particular roles. It's often easier to frame most challenges by asking, "In what ways can we. . . ." They fill in the blank by thinking about possible answers to the question. This introspective moment with your team members is called *Green Light Thinking*, just as a green traffic light triggers cars to move forward.

During this step in the Green Light Thinking exercise, Hannah's team sat quietly for several minutes and wrote down their individual lists of potential Coffee Stains that they knew their customers were experiencing from the inbound calls they received.

Step 2: Create a List

Go around the room and have everyone share what they wrote, writing their answers on a whiteboard, flip chart, or somewhere that everyone involved can see the list. Be sure to number each item as you go. Duplicate ideas are to be expected, and that is fine. Simply acknowledge the nuance in the answer and combine it with the similar, previously shared response. Make sure the group agrees that it is, in fact, the same issue or concept.

Throughout this process, Hannah and her team uncovered a number of potential Coffee Stains that may have an impact on the organization's customer experience. Everything from the packaging they used to late shipments to the number of repeated questions and concerns they received from the same clients were listed as potential Coffee Stains for their clients. In all, they came up with a list of nine Coffee Stains to explore.

Step 3: Do a Little Math

You are going to do a little math in this step, and the way it works is this: Take the number of items that you have on your list, divide it by 3, and then add 1. Hannah's team had nine total items on their list, so she divided 9 by 3, and then added 1 to come up with 4 ($9 \div 3 + 1 = 4$).

Step 4: Vote Based on the Product of Step 3

Everyone gets to vote on the items on the list that they believe should be the top priority for the organization. Each person gets votes equal to the number you arrived at in step 3. Give everyone 2 minutes to take a look at the list you have created together and write down their votes. Each person on Hannah's team picked their top four items that they believed were the most important to address in the organization to improve their customers' experiences.

Step 5: Tally the Votes and Select Priority

Finally, tally the group's votes by counting individual votes for each numbered item or idea on the group list. A simple way to count votes is to ask the members of your group to raise their hands as you go down the list written on the whiteboard or flip chart. Write the number of votes that each list item has received. You will typically end up with consensus around one, maybe two, top issues.

Throughout this process, Hannah's team identified that repeat calls from customers with additional questions and issues was their number one Coffee Stain. Together, they determined that if they could formalize a method of asking the right questions to try to make sure they were addressing all the customer's issues the first time, they predicted that they could reduce the number of incoming calls and improve the customer experience.

This led the team to launch their "What Else?" program. **Whenever the customer support staff engaged a client, they began to ask, "What questions do** you have? What else can we help you with?" This proactive inquiry led to more effective communication with customers, helping to build relationships that encourage repeat business. This success bred more success, and they repeated the ⅓ + 1 Method to generate 20 more ideas. The consensus from this session was to apply what the team referred to as a "Follow-Up, Follow-Through" initiative to improve the experience of their customers.

"Follow-Up, Follow-Through" meant that account managers would proactively call customers at predetermined milestones to follow up and make sure that the organization was following through on whether they were meeting customer expectations, particularly by keeping the promises made by the sales department. This initiative achieved three things for the organization. First, it improved cross-departmental communication between the inside sales engineers responsible for spare parts and the account managers. Second, it increased customer dialogue to help the accounts team identify Coffee Stains that they could quickly rectify to improve customer experiences. Third, and perhaps most astonishingly, it contributed almost entirely to the organization's 56 percent sales increase over 12 months.

The ⅓ + 1 Method is a practical tool that you can use repeatedly with your teams to create consensus and get buy-in. This process provides you with a prioritized list of items that will eventually need to be addressed, but not everything can be done at once. By isolating the top one or two priorities through the ⅓ + 1 approach, your team is more likely to focus their energy on true, immediate priorities. Your team will operate more efficiently, working together toward a common purpose. **Your team will be more committed to the execution of solving the issue because they were greatly involved in the process of identifying it and coming up with solutions.** This process helps facilitate open dialogue and creates consensus among the team about what items need to be prioritized and the manner in which they should be addressed.

The ⅓ + 1 Method

Step 1: Green Light Thinking.

Step 2: Create a list of Coffee Stains (or a different problem to solve together).

Step 3: Add up number of Coffee Stains, divide by 3, and then add 1.

Step 4: Vote based on the product of step 3.

Step 5: Tally the votes.

Hannah found that, by using the $\frac{1}{3}$ + 1 Method, she could open up communication within her team. Because the members knew they had a welcome voice and influence over how they could improve their own tasks, and because they saw the positive results of the initiatives they drove, Hannah's team gained greater confidence in airing customer complaints and the organization's Coffee Stains while also taking responsibility for correction by bringing their own ideas for remedies to the group. They became more engaged in innovating operations and motivated to execute new initiatives, and Hannah was able to move from a manager who had to tell and direct her team to meet expectations to a leader who could influence her team to engage in a dialogue to improve customer experience.

> If you lost your title of authority, would you still be effective in influencing other team members?

Negotiation and Building Consensus

One of the reasons bees communicate so well is that each individual works together with others as one unit. Bees have no need for negotiation or building consensus. In the human workspace, leaders need to be able to influence individuals through negotiation and consensus-building both within the organization and without.

For many people, negotiation conjures images of combativeness and partially truthful dealings. But the truth is that negotiation is a key tool in leveraging influence both within the organization as well as externally with vendors and clients, and it requires open and effective communication. **Perhaps no other leadership skill offers a greater chance to make an immediate, bottom-line impact on your organization and career than negotiation.**

Leela, the chief strategy officer and chief risk officer for an insurance provider based in the Caribbean, proved this through saving her organization $2.5 million by applying the negotiation skills she had honed through her leadership development training to two major deals. Leela already had mergers and acquisitions in her portfolio, and it was the part of her job that really excited her. When she realized that she would be attending classes during her leadership course that focused on negotiation strategy and tactics, she was skeptical, thinking to herself, "I have negotiated so many deals. Why should I give up my time to just be told what I already know?"

Leela was surprised to discover she picked up tips that she had not known before, and was delighted by the opportunity to focus her attention on tried-and-true negotiation tactics to hone her skills.

Negotiation Tactic 1: Focus on Needs and Interests

Leela found herself working on two negotiations that were big deals for her organization. The first was with a vendor who had submitted a proposal to help the organization build a robust new online customer management system. It was a big project that Leela and the rest of the leadership team knew would be a great asset to their organization, once completed, but they were looking at making a very large investment upfront to get the project going. She knew that, rather than going into a negotiation with an us-versus-them mentality, she should start by focusing on the interests and needs of all parties rather than simply on her position.

Visualize a pie with party A on one side and party B on the other side. If that is a fixed pie, then the process of the negotiation is simply dividing that pie. But that makes it a win–lose situation because anything A gets, B loses, and vice versa. Most negotiations that you may be involved in are not fixed pies, but instead can be expanded by understanding the other party's interests and needs as well as your interests and needs. By taking specific interests and needs into perspective, we are better able to work something out to expand the pie and create a win–win scenario for both parties.

By understanding both of your needs and interests, you are also better equipped to use relative value to your advantage. This allows you to make concessions on things that cost you relatively little in terms of time, money, or effort but have a high value for the other party. It works on the flip side as well; think about asking for things that might be relatively easy for the other party to provide while presenting a greater value to your interests and needs.

There is a common parable that often is used to explain fairness and negotiation. There are several versions, but it basically goes something like this. Two children were fighting over the last orange in the house. Both wanted the orange, but there was only one. The wise parent fetched a knife and instructed one child to cut the orange in half and the other child to choose between the two halves. Peace was restored in their home, and we can learn an important lesson from the parable.

But, considering that negotiations are not normally fixed pies and considering the interests and needs of the children, was this the best solution to the problem? Not necessarily. Did any of the three characters take the time to look beyond the position to see if there was a way to expand the size of the pie by focusing on the children's needs and interests? The fact that both children needed the orange and there was only one is the position, but what if one of them only wanted the fruit from the orange and the other needed just the peel as zest for baking? If they had focused on the needs and interests of both parties, each would have gotten twice as much.

Similar to not focusing on position, **refrain from getting hung up on one item in a negotiation.** There are always ways to get to other terms and conditions that will help expand the pie and get a win for both parties.

Leela knew that her organization would really benefit from the development and maintenance of this new customer management system—there was much to gain from making this investment. But she was also aware that the developers would benefit significantly from working with an organization of their size and prominence in the area. It would also mean a new foothold in the insurance services industry that could open more doors for the developers. She knew that they would be entering a partnership in which both organizations stood to benefit from. Knowing this, she leveraged their individual needs and interests during their negotiations.

Negotiation Tactic 2: Understand the Difference Between Authority and Power

A common mistake in negotiations is assuming you have greater power because you have more authority. As a matter of fact, many times the contrary is the case. Power in negotiations can come from being an agent of limited authority. Being an agent of limited authority means that there is always a higher authority you need to check with before making decisions and concessions. This allows you to use time to your advantage, ensuring that you do not just jump on the first offer or concede too quickly. It gives you time and space to come back with a counteroffer, while the other party ideally is wondering if their offer was fair. Being an agent of limited authority also helps you maintain a good relationship in a negotiation because it is always someone else who is being the bad guy and saying no.

The balance of power in negotiations is not about who has the authority, but rather who is perceived to have the power. Doing your homework to fully understand your needs and interests, as well as those of the other party, creates a level of power that most likely only you know about. People generally tend to underestimate their level of power in a negotiation situation. Know that you probably have more power than you think and take that into account. When you believe you have less power, you are less likely to take risks. The ability to take calculated risks in negotiations also creates power. Be willing to walk away from a deal rather than sit at the table until the bitter end.

A popular tactic in creating power in a negotiation is to play the part of a reluctant seller or buyer. As a reluctant seller, your goal is to get the best or highest selling price. As a reluctant buyer, you are negotiating for the best or lowest buying price. Either role is meant to create negotiation power by not coming across as being too eager for the deal.

Another great way to create power in a negotiation is to ask questions. A great question to ask is something along the lines of, "Is there anything else that I should know regarding this matter?" The response to this question may or may not be materially important to you, but what it does is it gets them thinking. They start second-guessing themselves, questioning whether there is something that you'll find out later. There are many scenarios in which different power questions will help you in your negotiations. Think about questions that would be effective in each of your individual negotiations.

Because Leela is a top-level executive, she wanted to downplay her perceived authority in making the final decision on the deal, so she took the simple step of needing to check back with her project team on offers from the developers. She did work with others on the leadership team, and the project managers who would be involved in the new system, to make sure that they were getting all the functionality and support that they would need. This helped her take a time out and get the other party to wait it out. She also asked a lot of questions: "What will be the extent of ongoing support?" "Can you send me your service level agreement?" "How can we adjust this agreement to reduce response time to 12 hours rather than 24?" and so on.

Negotiation Tactic 3: Talk Less and Listen More

Asking power questions will help you talk less and listen more, and is another great way to create power in a negotiation. The reality is that you can always tell who has the power in a negotiation scenario by who is doing the talking and who is doing the listening. When you talk too much, you start assuming things about the other party—and when you start assuming what the other party wants, you end up giving away too much in concessions. **When you get the other party to talk more, you now have a negotiation edge.** Use this knowledge to your advantage and restate their points to your advantage.

Ask probing questions, and answer questions with a question. For example, if someone were to ask you, "What are you prepared to give me?" a highly effective response is simply, "What do you think is fair?"

This question gets the other party talking, prevents you from assuming that you know what the other party wants, while also leveraging their sense of integrity and fairness. This exchange helps to lay the groundwork from which both parties can construct a fair and mutually beneficial agreement.

Negotiation Tactic 4: Never Concede Too Quickly

Be prepared to take risks, particularly the smaller ones, because the biggest mistake most people make is jumping at a first offer. You are then left wondering if you got the best deal that you possibly could have negotiated. We go into a negotiation with a specific figure in mind. Sometimes, the initial offer is much better than we thought we would get and, in an instant, we decide to simply go for it rather than drag out negotiations. Instead, **be patient and prepared to go through the whole negotiation process.**

As a veteran negotiator, Leela and the developers did go back and forth with offers several times until they finally settled on the price. Finally, Leela submitted what she told them would be her final counter. The developers responded, "Okay, we will think about it and get back to you." The next day, they came back with yet another counteroffer. When she brought their counteroffer to the project team they asked, "What do you think we should do, the counter is good?"

Undeterred, Leela knew how much the developers needed the project and the revenue that would come with it, so she advised, "Yes the counter is good, it's within our budget and our tolerance level, but I know we can do better on this. No, I say we stick with our final counteroffer and make sure they know we are serious."

So, Leela and her team held their ground, "No, you are going to have to do better. We are sticking with our final counteroffer."

This is called using the *vise technique*. Think of how a vise works: when you turn the lever, two jaws come together and work to hold an object tightly in place. The vise technique places pressure on the other party. You will be surprised by the impact that this simple statement, "You'll have to do better than this" will have. An experienced or savvy negotiator will respond with, "Well, exactly how much better will I have to do?" However, often the other party will concede a big chunk of their negotiating range just because of that statement.

And it absolutely worked for Leela and the project team. Leela was a bit nervous, but she felt confident that the vise technique she had learned during her leadership development training would work. Two days later, the developers came back and accepted her offer $500,000 lower than they had tried to counteroffer. Leela and her team were elated! Not only had they saved a significant amount of money on the project, but they had experienced applying their new negotiation skills as a team to have a great impact on their organization.

Leela's negotiation did not come down to this, but it is also important to **resist the temptation to concede by offering to split the difference.** That is not to say that you can't agree to split the difference, but keep the high ground in the negotiation by attempting to draw it out from the other party. This goes back to the point about maintaining power. When you offer to split the difference, you are giving the power and the control to the other party. For example, if you are at 90 percent and the other party is at 100 percent and you offer to split the difference at 95 percent, what happens? The other party has held the high ground, they are still at 100 percent and you have brought yourself up to 95 percent. They have the power.

Negotiation Tactic 5: Focus on Creating Consensus to Build the Relationship

Many negotiations have the tendency to become highly emotional. If you were to study negotiations, you would find that many of them are lost because someone was backed into a corner and there was no way to save face. This goes back to understanding the other party's needs and interests to find ways to make sure that the negotiation results in a win–win consensus that builds the relationship.

Leela's second negotiation was an acquisition that became quite emotional for the other party. They were working toward acquiring a smaller competitor that represented a strategic move into a new geographic market for the organization. The owner of the smaller insurance organization had spent his entire adult life building the business from the ground up. He was very personally and emotionally attached to the business. Leela enjoyed reaching out and connecting with the man on a personal level. This was an acquisition that would include him in the ongoing operations of the location, and she wanted to make sure that the negotiation experience was a positive one to nurture their future relationship.

You can succeed at building the relationship by following the Platinum Rule, in other words, treating people the way *they* want to be treated. The Golden Rule says "Do unto others as you would have them do unto you." The problem with the Golden Rule is that is puts the emphasis on you. You're treating everybody the way you want to be treated, but people are different. It's better to treat them according to the Platinum Rule, **"Do unto others as they would have you do unto them."** This plays into the technique of *mirroring*, with which you mirror the other person's style, pace, mannerisms, and language.

Part of treating people the way they want to be treated is accepting that, in any emotional situation, which could include negotiation situations, feelings need to be treated as facts. If the other party feels a certain way, you have to accept that as a fact. It's not a question of whether or not they *should* feel that way. They *do* feel that way. When the other party is starting to get hostile, hurt, or injured, you need to accept that emotion and empathize with them. You do not need to assume responsibility for their feelings, but you can show that you accept their feelings and can understand where they are coming from. The ability to express empathy will greatly help your ability to maintain a positive relationship with the other party rather than allowing it to turn negative. **Rarely should you respond to hostility with hostility.**

When you get hostile and put on a combative posture, you're automatically triggering the other person's natural fight-or-flight mechanism. People will either want to walk away from the deal or they'll respond in kind by becoming aggressive or defensive. Instead, never take personal offense in negotiation. When you get offended, it can only work to your detriment. Instead of letting things get negative and hostile, good negotiators always come to a consensus on how they are going to resolve differences ahead of time, and they always go into any negotiation with alternatives in mind in case the negotiation falls through. **Deciding how to resolve differences may include involving the other party in that decision at the beginning**. You might say, "Our good relationship is important, so let's define how we should best proceed if we do not reach an agreement. Would you consider using a third party to assist us in the process or decision?"

When the owner of the insurance business that was being acquired submitted his first offer, Leela asked him questions to understand how he came to his offer. After a bit of discussion, he began to open up more about his personal attachment to the business. Their conversation gave her a deeper understanding of the details that, from his perspective, created the value that made him come to his pricing decision. He was feeling sadness about letting his business go. He compared it to a child who you raise and nurture, and who one day has grown into an adult—and you have to let the child go on to bigger and better things. He wanted to see the business do well, but he was feeling sad about giving up ownership.

Leela used the **feel, felt, found technique**, also often used in sales to comfort the business owner.

"I understand how you **feel**," explained Leela. "We just finished solidifying another partnership whose owner **felt** the same way you do. This business is your legacy, and you are looking at giving up a big part of you. But, you know what? Our other partner **found** that he could only take his business to a certain level and that if he wanted his business to realize its full potential he had to let others in."

This position moved the conversation from being a mere transaction to a personal discussion about how their relationship wasn't just about money. It was about creating a partnership and building a relationship that would help the owner realize his dream for his business. He connected with this and, through their discussions, eventually brought his selling price down by $2 million.

You can't win the negotiation game if the other side feels like they've lost. Part of your responsibility in negotiation is to create a consensus that all parties are getting what they need out of the deal to build the relationship. Remember, negotiation is not a fixed pie. By understanding interests and needs, empathizing, and creating consensus, you can expand that pie to find a win–win scenario that helps build the relationship.

Do you negotiate to win, or do you use your process to strengthen relationships in which both parties feel valued and both win?

Emotional Intelligence

Emotional intelligence, also referred to as EQ or EI, is the act of knowing, understanding, and responding to emotions; overcoming stress in the moment; and being aware of how your words and actions affect others. Emotional intelligence is commonly referred to as a soft skill, but developing a high **EI gives you a competitive edge in your ability to influence and lead your team—what we call a soft edge.** When you have high EI, your ability to recognize verbalized or unspoken feelings can empower you to be more sensitive to timing and to better manage the words and the tone of the words that come out of your mouth.

There are four key attributes that contribute to the measurement and development of emotional intelligence. These are (1) self-awareness, (2) self-management, (3) social awareness, and (4) relationship management. Leaders who have a high degree of self-awareness are able to identify their own personal motivators, emotions, and triggers as different situations arise. They accept themselves for who they are—although truly effective leaders never stop striving to become better or understand their personal strengths and weaknesses.

When leaders are strong in self-management, they can control their emotions and behaviors. They don't react emotionally to changing circumstances and are resilient in the face of challenges. In addition, great self-managers are strong in balancing their priorities and commitments, while also implementing strategies for personal growth.

Social awareness includes the ability to recognize the emotional cues in others and empathize with them. **Socially aware leaders understand the dynamics of power and influence in a group and are aware of their personal surroundings, audience, and environment and how they may need to adjust differently to these variations.** They also realize how they can positively affect others in ways that are specifically meaningful.

Strong relationship management requires that a leader is capable of inspiring and influencing others. Leaders can communicate and execute their vision while developing positive relationships. They build the right team around them, mentor and grow their team, and work toward creating team consensus on executing the vision. They build trust and credibility through integrity.

All four attributes of emotional intelligence are equally important, and they are not sequential. For example, you do not necessarily need to fully develop your self-awareness before moving into self-management. Most people will find that they are strong in some areas and lacking in others. Reflecting on and identifying your own emotional intelligence strengths and weaknesses is the first step to developing more EI. But developing your EI doesn't just happen overnight. It takes time, commitment, and dedication to improve those weaker areas of emotional intelligence while also improving in areas that already are your strengths.

> Is emotional intelligence your soft edge—do you build productive relationships by leveraging your emotional intelligence?

Influencing others is the primary mechanism through which great leaders lead. Although it is tempting for some to lead through authority, this approach results in limited organizational success. Under an authoritarian approach, team members will ultimately only accomplish the bare minimum of what is expected, resulting in limited success and growth for the organization. Using open and effective communication, negotiation and building consensus, and emotional intelligence are the leadership tools that allow a great leader to influence greatness and excellence in the work that is executed by his or her team.

Core Competency: Influences Others

Listens and fosters open communication through questioning, dialogue, and information-sharing. Advocates ideas and effectively negotiates to achieve mutually successful outcomes. Identifies and proactively manages own emotions.

Competency Skills
- **Open and Effective Communication:** Listens and fosters open communication through questioning, dialogue, and information-sharing
- **Negotiation and Building Consensus:** Advocates ideas and effectively negotiates to achieve mutually successful outcomes
- **Emotional Intelligence:** Builds productive relationships by managing emotions and practices social awareness of other's emotions

---

Influences Others Assessment Questions

1. During your one-on-one sessions with your employees, do you often talk more than listen?
2. If you lost your title of authority, would you still be effective in influencing other team members?
3. Do you negotiate to win, or do you use your process to strengthen relationships in which both parties feel valued and both win?

4. Is emotional intelligence your soft edge—do you build productive relation-ships by leveraging your emotional intelligence?

The Leader's Toolkit

1. During your next team meeting, use the $\frac{1}{3}$ +1 Method. Obtain feedback from your team members about how they felt about the process and the meeting. Did they feel their voices were heard?

The $\frac{1}{3}$ + 1 Method

Step 1: Green Light Thinking.

Step 2: Create a list of Coffee Stains.

Step 3: Add up number of Coffee Stains, divide by 3, and then add 1.

Step 4: Vote based on the product of step 3.

Step 5: Tally the votes.

---

2. During your next one-on-one session with your employees, practice asking questions versus telling. In fact, try to *only* ask questions and assess your results.

3. When employees are looking to you to solve an issue for them, first ask:

   a. What is your recommendation?

   b. What have you tried so far?

Through these questions, help them realize that they likely have already solved their own issue. Use this same approach in peer meetings and assess your effectiveness. You may find that the more questions you ask, the more influential you are. Remain genuinely curious.

Understands the Business

In the Middle Ages, people considered chicken soup an aphrodisiac. The market demand for sexual stimulants has been a business driver for enterprising individuals and organizations throughout time. But before you simmer small white dumplings with libido-boosting chicken broth, consider the many other entrées or ingredients thought of as aphrodisiacs at one time or another in history: clams, oysters, eggs, celery, and stimulating avocados, to name a few.

In December 2015, *The Economist* magazine published a story about a Tibetan love drug called *yartsa gunbu*. It is a fungus, and the business of gathering and selling yartsu gunbu, according to *The Economist*, has brought "unprecedented wealth to rural Tibet."[2] In a 10-year span, the return on sales of yartsu gunbu has climbed more than 17 times its original price. Sharp business acumen can stimulate higher revenues, regardless of the product or service.

Generates Business Insights

Organizations thrive when their leaders grasp the financial impact of every decision, whether it is a small operation in the Tibetan Plateau or a much larger team of managers elsewhere in the world. The ability of managers to generate business insights and to improve productivity and process efficiencies can be and should be developed through training and experience.

Business acumen is the understanding of how the business operates, makes money, and grows profitably. It is a skill that everyone in your organization needs to develop. **Business acumen is everyone's business,** not just the accounting or finance department's responsibility. It is important that you understand how your department fits into the big picture and how it contributes to the success and

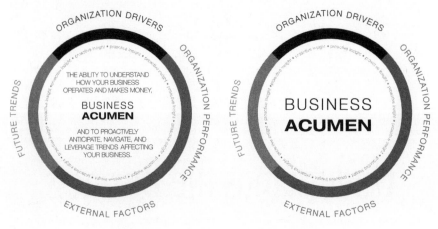

Figure 4.1   Business Acumen Model

profitability of the organization. It is just as important to ensure that all team members are aware of the ways they directly or indirectly affect organization finances and measured goals.

Every business and organization's ability to grow profitably is affected by the four key elements of business acumen: (1) organizational drivers, (2) organizational performance, (3) external factors, and (4) future trends. Managers with business acumen also have insight to proactively anticipate, navigate, and leverage trends affecting the business.

Organizational Drivers

> Do your employees understand how they affect the business and how they create business value?

Organizational drivers are factors that create value for your organization, and there are many. Organizational drivers vary by industry, but they will generally fall into similar clusters, including people, revenue, operational efficiency, product, and quality. A common example of an organizational driver is customer experience. A positive customer experience has great potential to drive organizational value, and it is a driver that everyone in the organization affects on some level, whether he or she is a front-line employee or in other areas of operations. Each functional area of the organization has an impact on your customers' experiences with your brand.

Everyone at every level in the organization has an impact on the growth (or lack thereof) of the organization. Communicate and reinforce the importance of every

Figure 4.2   Organizational Driver Models.

team member's role to the success of creating value through organizational drivers by creating an Organizational Drivers Model for your organization. For each key driver affecting your organization, map out how each employee's position affects that specific driver. The middle of the model is the manager position. Surrounding the middle, write the position or title for each person or team within your area of responsibility and describe how they directly or indirectly affect that driver.

Understanding the drivers that affect your organization, and how each position influences those drivers, helps focus your thinking on the key drivers as well as on current and future trends that may affect your organization's ability to create value, grow, and remain competitive. Your ability to recognize, understand, and leverage these trends contributes to the long-term, strategic success of your organization.

Organizational Performance

Are your performance goals for your employees tangible and measurable, and do they tie to the organization's key drivers?

Understanding how your team affects the overall performance of the organization is too important to be left solely to the finance department. Each role and department affects the performance of the organization. As a result, individuals need to understand how they affect their department's budget. Individual performance goals must link to the success of the organization overall, for example, how team members will drive awareness and sales to help reach organizational revenue goals.

Fresh water is a difficult commodity to come by on the Arabian Peninsula, so much so that approximately 50 percent of the fresh water supply in Saudi Arabia comes from desalination. Desalination, wastewater treatment, and water distribution all have been increasingly outsourced to private companies by the Saudi government since the early 2000s. The government regularly purchases fresh water from these private desalination organizations and sells it to its citizens for almost nothing. Omar, a foreman at a water desalination and distribution utility organization in Saudi Arabia, had little financial background and certainly was not expected to balance the books. But what he did have was an intimate understanding of how the organization's desalination, distribution, and wastewater processes worked—an understanding that led him to start wondering how they could improve an inefficiency that had been nagging at him for some time. He wanted to start reusing at least some of the wastewater that the organization simply dumped after the desalination treatment was complete.

Omar began researching what other organizations were doing, and what new innovations were being developed that could help potentially monetize the wastewater that was currently being dumped. What he found was that other organizations were learning how to store and reuse the byproduct wastewater from desalination—referred to as graywater—for uses such as irrigation, cleaning, and restrooms. Omar brought this information to the management team, who recognized his great idea. The organization purchased storage tanks made specifically for storing graywater, an innovation that saved the organization SAR 13,000 every month from reduced internal water usage.

Omar's proactive thinking has made a definite impact on the organization's bottom line in water use savings, and also has the potential to create future revenue with additional investments and innovations. Omar characterized why business acumen is urgent and important for everyone in your organization to develop. You can begin encouraging this at every level of your organization by starting with each department's financials.

Each department has financial indicators that they should use to track and measure the impact they are having on the organization's performance. For example, a manufacturing plant manager will likely use indicators such as process waste level, inventory shrinkage rate, quality index, and process or machine downtime to assess how the manufacturing department is performing. A sales and marketing manager is not going to be too concerned with these measurements, but for his or her department the manager will be analyzing market share, brand equity, cost per lead, and customer complaints and satisfaction. The leadership team needs to work with department managers to make the determination regarding which **performance indicators are most important and relevant to measuring departmental goals, as well as providing the best indication of how the department is contributing to organizational goals.**

External Factors

Leaders need to be aware of changing external factors and how those external factors affect their organization. External factors are things that happen outside of your organization over which you have no control. Examples of external factors include: regulations, politics, economic conditions, customer requirements, and competitors. External factors have the ability to threaten as well as present new opportunities to your organization. It is not enough to simply understand and be aware of these factors. Leaders also need to be innovative, proactive thinkers to mitigate potential threats and leverage new opportunities that external factors may create.

What are the most significant external factors affecting your business? Do you ask the bigger questions of your employees about the business?

Future Trends

Future trends with the ability to affect your business include competitive, regulatory, socioeconomic, environmental, technological, and customer market trends. To prepare to leverage these trends, first ask yourself: How scalable is your organization and how difficult is it to enter your market?

It is very easy for organizations today to get blindsided by the future, and part of this issue is scalability and competition. We are seeing businesses scale up faster than ever before in history. For example, it took over 200 years for the first billion bicycles to be sold in the world, 23 years for McDonald's to sell its first billion hamburgers, 5½ years for Uber to sell the first billion rides, and just 11 months for Uber's competitor in China, Didi Chuxing, to sell its first billion rides—just within China!

No industry is safe. Today, it is entirely possible to lose market dominance to a competitor that did not exist months or even weeks ago. The call to action may be quick scalability to own the market. Think about how your organization can simplify and streamline its offerings for fast growth without cannibalizing its key brands.

Leverage your knowledge of your market, given the trends of the future and your perspective of the past, to understand your organization's market position. Is your organization or team well positioned today to take advantage of the future trends, or are you in trouble? Do you need to make some key changes now to ensure that your organization or team will sustain and thrive in the future? Are you keeping an open perspective, or are you closing your mind to possible opportunities and competitive surprises?

Managers, like most people, tend to rely greatly on the way things have been done in the past, especially if those things have contributed profitably to the viability of the organization. They tend to focus on past experiences rather than anticipating an unknown future. This is a mistake that can quickly lead organizations and today's decisions to irrelevance in the marketplace. Instead, envision several possible scenarios for your organization's future path. **Your vision of the future defines the decisions you make today,** so make sure that your vision is clear and that you have thought of possible contingencies. Work toward achieving that vision by acting on the future now to follow the path you and your organization need to take to get you there. Today's leadership decisions and actions matter to your organization's short- and long-term future.

One of the actions you need to make today to ensure your organization's future sustainability includes defining the new skills and competencies that you and your team should be learning today to position yourself and your organization to have a competitive edge. **The skills that employees need now and will continue to need in the future include the ability to be flexible and agile,** while at the same time be focused on producing results and getting things done in a rapidly changing environment. Work now toward positioning your team for success by providing opportunities to grow by developing new skills and refining the knowledge and skills members already have.

> Are you encouraging and allowing your employees to be innovative and curious?

To maintain a successful business for over 40 years, a transportation and shipping organization based in Hong Kong has long understood the value of taking a long-term approach to investing in developing the skills of their management team. The organization's continued growth was being challenged by not developing a pipeline of upcoming new leaders needed for the organization to effectively respond to transitions and to generate fresh, new ideas. They recognized this deficiency and, looking ahead, knew that to build their future executive team, a higher standard of business acumen training was required for their management team. It would need to cover all areas of management, including recruitment, business development, and compliance—along with strong commercial insights to enable the necessary return on investment for the organization. They made leadership training compulsory for all managers whose skills development percolated down through the junior management team, as well as the rest of the organization.

They selected a leadership development program with a reputation as a trusted, comprehensive, and accountability-focused program. Investing in the program enabled them to measure improvements in productivity, efficiency, customer satisfaction, and communication. It was no coincidence that two senior leadership positions were subsequently filled by two managers who had participated in the leadership development training program.

Their return on investment from having developed the future skills of their managers is greater organization profitability today. The organization has been able to attract and retain business dealings from blue-chip customers, such as Goodyear and IKEA, in part because of their reputation for being an organization that develops its team from the bottom up. This has ensured quality service on multimillion contracts that are no longer awarded on price alone. Those kinds of customer relationships require a commitment to service and excellence that many in their industry struggle to achieve by competing merely on price.

The organization's customers recognize that their transportation partners form an integral part of their supply chain and represent their business. They value the quality of the service that is directly affected by the capability and leadership skills of the organization's management team.

The financial returns on their leadership development investment now exceed millions of dollars. This transportation and shipping organization grew 11 percent in sales and 50 percent in profit over the past year, which it strongly attributed to the foresight it had to develop the management team's skills and strengthen the leadership pipeline. The organization recognized the competitive advantage that leadership development could provide and took the initiative to seize that advantage.

> What global trends will affect your organization, and how will you navigate or leverage?

Financial Management

Generating business insights relies heavily on understanding and managing the financial performance of your organization. Managing financial performance is too important to be left alone to the chief financial officer. All leaders must have a basic understanding of financials and department budgets.

Every business is in business to make money, and it is your financial statements that tell the story of how you do that. **Learning the language of finance opens new insights for you** into what is working in your organization and what is not, how you are performing based on historical data and in real time, and provides the financial information you need to make the right investment decisions for the future of your organization.

Key performance indicators (KPIs) are figures that help you assess the performance of your organization. Examples of commonly used KPIs include net profit margin, gross profit margin, earnings before interest, taxes, depreciation and amortization, revenue growth rate, return on investment, return on assets and equity, and debt-to-equity ratio, just to name a few. Nonprofit organizations may track performance metrics such as donor number growth, donation growth, and donor retention rate. The same applies to public sector organizations that may measure things such as percent of programs exceeding their evaluation goals or the ratio of operating costs to budget. Often represented as a ratio, **KPIs help tell the story of how your organization is performing financially, as well as how you might adapt or adjust to trends.**

Laura was a customer service manager for a mid-sized industrial printing and publishing organization in Canada. Although her organization routinely tracked a wide range of KPIs, she focused heavily on a measurement called net promoter score (NPS), first introduced and trademarked by Frederick Reichheld, Satmetrix, and Bain & Company. This KPI measures customer loyalty and often is viewed as an indicator of future repeat and new customers.

Custom printing had become competitive in Laura's market, and the pressure to dominate the market motivated her to constantly assess the effectiveness of her team to grow her organization's competitive advantage. Since being hired for the position 1 year before, she had been prompt in asking questions and determining ways that her team could measure customer trends. Search engine rankings and click-through rates, as well as customer online engagement levels, provided useful data, but ultimately her team was interested in the likelihood of their customers to buy again and recommend the organization's services to their friends.

By asking customers to rate on a scale of 0 to 10 how likely they were to recommend the business to others and why they had chosen that rating, Laura's team gathered valuable insight into an issue that needed to be resolved.

Customers shared both positive and negative feedback about the responsiveness and support provided by more than one department in the organization. By calculating the scores given by customers, Laura realized the need to pass along her findings to senior leaders. Customers collectively had indicated a breakdown in the organization's communication, which appeared to have occurred because different departments in the organization had failed to talk with one another regarding a consistent range of customer issues.

By measuring customer experience, Laura was able to recommend changes in the way managers worked together to improve customer support. Within 15 months, organization-wide improvements had not only raised the NPS score significantly but had directly led to a 34 percent increase in annual customer spend.

No single KPI tells the whole story. Rather, leaders and managers rely on a several KPIs to understand the big picture. Some KPIs will make the organization look like it is performing very well, while others will show a less optimistic picture. Analyzing and understanding KPIs is key to successfully managing organization or department finances. Different companies, or different industries, focus on and give greater weight to different KPIs that are most relevant to them.

Cash flow is perhaps the most important KPI that every business manager should at least be aware of. Most nonfinancial managers assume that cash flow is more or less equivalent to profit. This is not true. Revenue is realized at the point of sale rather than when money is collected, and expenses are matched to revenue during a given income statement period rather than when it is paid. Capital investments also create the difference between cash flow and profit because you would have paid for that capital investment with cash, but capital investments are not counted against profit. To say that cash flow equals profit is false, but the truth is easy to explain and understand by managers at every level.

Cash flow is defined as either an *inflow* or an *outflow* organized into three categories: (1) operating activities, (2) investing activities, and (3) financing activities. Cash flow in/from operating activities shows how well the organization is able to use profits to generate growth internally, without needing to leverage assets. Cash flow in/from investing activities shows how much an organization is investing cash in future growth. Cash flow in/from financing activities gives insight regarding how dependent the organization is on financing activities, or if it is able to pay for growth from internal profits.

> "Cash is king" is an expression sometimes used in analyzing businesses or
> investment portfolios. It refers to the importance of cash flow in
> the overall fiscal health of a business.

Once you have a better understanding how cash flow works, you are in a better position to help manage your effect on your organization's cash position. You can make better informed, more proactive decisions regarding the timing of purchases, inventory control, and extending lines of credit based on your knowledge of the organization's cash position. This helps keep your organization in a strong financial position while also displaying your understanding of the business.

Productivity and Process Efficiency

Productivity and *efficiency* are terms that sometimes are incorrectly used interchangeably. Productivity is determined by the amount of output produced during a set period of time, whereas efficiency is more concerned with the quality of the output. Some companies measure output based on productivity efficiency or efficient productivity, which takes both of these concepts into account. This results in a net output, which subtracts faulty and rejected product from the total amount of output (productivity) during a period of time.

Processes are meant to help improve productivity efficiency by defining steps to ensure that tasks are done correctly and consistently. It has been argued that process is actually the antithesis of productivity. In truth, a process can be productivity's best friend or worst enemy, depending on the efficiency of process requirements.

If a process has too much red tape—approval checks and balances—that red tape gets in the way of accomplishing even the simplest tasks in a reasonable amount of time, your process is inefficient and is working against the productivity of your organization. However, processes that are working well have a great ability to streamline tasks to improve efficiency and productivity.

Productivity and process efficiency are important aspects of understanding the big picture of how the organization creates value. Let's say that you become aware that one of your competitors can sell its product at a price that is 25 percent less than your best price. The likely reason is because your competitor can produce, ship, or distribute the product at a more efficient rate; therefore, it has a lower overhead and can pass those savings along to customers to create value and strategic advantage. This leads you to realize that you need to focus your efforts on improving process efficiency and productivity in your own organization to remain competitive and relevant.

A software engineer, a hardware engineer, and a department manager were on their way to an off-site meeting. While driving down a steep road, the brakes on their car failed. The car swerved into a guardrail, crushing one side of the car and shattering one of the windows as the wrecked car soon came to a full stop at the bottom of a long hill. The three managers were shaken but unhurt. Once calm, they discussed what to do.

"I know," said the department manager, "let's have a meeting, define some goals, and then execute a process of continuous improvement to find a solution to the critical problems . . . and we can be on our way."

"Absolutely not," said the hardware engineer. "That will take too long, and, besides, we have these tools we could use to strip down the car's braking system, isolate the problem, fix it, and we can be on our way."

"Well," said the software engineer, "before we do anything, I think we should push the car back up the road and see if it happens again."

Everyone has processes, and how things may get done often develops from the available tools, competence, and point of view of those involved. As a matter of fact, good processes are frequently developed precisely because of the perspective, experience, and tools of managers and talented employees.

Processes that may have been effective, fashionable, or even cutting-edge at one time may not be so now—and if not completely outdated, then trailing newer ways. When leaders or others say words like, "That's the way it's always been done," this or similar statements refer to processes. Forward-thinking leaders have the courage and commitment to regularly assess processes to capitalize on changes that have occurred in technology, consumer trends, and other factors.

Take a detailed look at each of the key processes in your organization that you believe affect key organizational drivers. Map out, step-by-step, what is occurring in each of these processes today. Specifically, you will want to map out who is doing what and where the handoffs from one process to another occur. While you are mapping out your processes, create a baseline for key metrics, such as how long it takes to go from one step to the next. Ensure you have balanced metrics to evaluate the new process changes. Metrics might include measurable outcomes, essentially goals such as *reducing order-to-shipment time by 1 day* or *improving customer satisfaction by 5 percent.*

How effective and efficient are the key business processes in your area?

Accountability and collaboration are key to effective process improvement. Review your process map with department heads and designate the process owners. **Every process should have one overall owner,** along with a group who will participate in the process improvement. Every person who touches the process in the group needs to be involved in the process redesign. During this review, highlight where the potential pain points, such as bottlenecks or inefficiencies, may be occurring. Brainstorm potential solutions to the inefficiencies with the group to ensure that you are collecting all the possible ideas and creating buy-in from the team. Assess what the potential savings and costs are for fixing the issues, and then create a project plan for implementation. Ensure that you are also doing a post audit after the new process has been implemented, and check your success metrics and your savings goals against those planned. Also assign the date when this process should be reviewed in the future.

Understanding the business requires the study of how internal and external factors interact to develop the big picture view of how the organization exists within the larger business environment. To understand the many facets of what creates business value to drive strategic advantage, managers must be able to generate business insights, practice financial management, influence productivity, and process efficiency improvements.

Core Competency: Understands the Business

Understands how businesses and organizations work. Applies knowledge of business drivers, financial indicators, and technology to generate productivity and insights.

Competency Skills
- **Generates Business Insights:** Uses knowledge of business drivers, trends, and how organizations make money to guide actions and generate insights
- **Financial Management:** Uses financial indicators and analysis to evaluate options and proactively manage financial results
- **Productivity and Process Efficiency:** Recognizes synergies and processes in need of improvement and makes suggestions to address problems

Understands the Business Assessment Questions

1. Do your employees understand how they affect the business and how they create business value?
2. Are your performance goals for your employees tangible and measurable, and do they tie to the organization's key drivers?
3. What are the most significant external factors affecting your business?
4. Do you ask the bigger questions of your employees about the business?
5. Are you encouraging and allowing your employees to be innovative and curious?
6. What global trends will affect your organization, and how will you navigate or leverage?
7. How effective and efficient are the key business processes in your area?

The Leader's Toolkit

1. Select members of your team to research current trends that affect your organization or department. Have these individuals present their findings to the large group and facilitate discussion around the trends in terms of their potential impact. Here is the recommended facilitation:

   a. Present an overview of the key trends to the large group.

b. Split the group up into two groups for discussion and have each group select a facilitator and a scribe.

c. Group 1 discusses: How could this trend positively affect our business? To what degree (1–10 high) could this trend affect our business positively? What action(s) do we recommend to leverage this trend?

d. Group 2 discusses: How could this trend negatively affect our business? To what degree (1–10 high) could this trend affect our business negatively? What action(s) do we recommend to mitigate the possible negative impacts of this trend?

e. Have each group present to one another and together determine what further actions (if any) should occur.

2. Review the glossary of financial terms in Appendix C with your team and assign a few key terms to each person (or groups of people for larger teams). At your next team meeting, have each of them present the term and how it specifically applies to your organization. You also may want to invite someone from the finance or accounting department to one of your team meetings to help educate your team on the basic financial terms and how they apply to your organization.

CHAPTER 5

Executes Vision

Das Auge sieht weit, der Verstand noch weiter may be a German expression, but its implication for leadership is universal. English speakers have a similar proverb: "The eye looks, but it is the mind that sees."

In October 1847, Werner von Siemens saw potential that others had not yet envisioned. His small workshop was the starting point for a vision of invention that would affect people on every continent. The German organization, now called Siemens AG, is recognized worldwide as the pioneer in electrical engineering and electronics. Its principal founder, Siemens, did more than imagine ways to revolutionize the use of electricity. He executed his vision.

Writers, executives, and historians may often associate remarkable business leaders, like Siemens, with their visions of growth and positive change. With Siemens, growth and change transformed the world. The organization, which started as a small team of engineers, has, through its growth, built the first underground railroad on the European continent, invented the world's first metal filament lamp, launched the European telephone network, and created the first supermicroscope—as well as the fingertip sensor technology commonly used today. These developments and more started as a seed planted in Siemens' mind. "The eye looks, but it is the mind that sees." The corollary to the *mind that sees* must be expressed as the *hands that act*. Vision becomes reality when organization leaders, even department managers and supervisors, act decisively on the blueprint.

Siemens' blueprint drove significant technological growth and transformational changes in the way people live and communicate. It built a new industry; yet, his vision—like the vision of many business leaders—was grounded in caring for his family. In the archives of Siemens AG, you will find a revealing letter from Werner von Siemens to his brother Carl.

"For me the business is only secondarily important as a source of wealth," he wrote. "I see it rather as a realm that I have founded and that I would like to pass on undiminished to my descendants so that they can continue to operate within it."[3]

A leader must be able to define the vision, strategy, and tactical plan for the organization to move forward, and then effectively communicate it to the team in a way that engages each team member and focuses the team around a common goal. Thinking strategically is a skill that can be learned, and leaders who develop this skill will create competitive advantage as they plan, prioritize, and execute what the mind alone can see.

Defines and Communicates Vision

What happens when you lead a team with no vision? Everyone ends up working, and often working quite hard, but important goals might not be achieved. A vision brings the team together under a common goal so that your team is not simply working but is working together toward something, to create something and to execute the vision.

The vision is a vivid, aspirational picture of the future of your organization. It is long-term and measurable. Your vision answers the question: Where are we going?

You need to be crystal clear in your definition of what that destination looks like, even if you do not yet know exactly how you are going to get there. This definition gives you and your team the ability to know exactly where you are located within the vision at any given time and whether you are getting closer to or further away from that destination. That destination must be exciting, not just to you and the people on your leadership team who may have helped you craft it, but also to the people who are charged with fulfilling it. **It is not enough to simply define a vision, you also must create buy-in from your team and your stakeholders to execute it.**

SpaceX is an aerospace organization with the vision to enable human life on Mars. There are many obstacles in the team's path to achieving that vision. Advances in human understanding and technology to sustain life on the trip to the red planet have not yet been accomplished. That does not deter individuals on the SpaceX team from trying because, as they put it on their website site, they were "founded under the belief that a future where humanity is out exploring the stars is fundamentally more exciting than one where we are not."[4] Inspiring? Absolutely.

Buy-in starts with how clear and exciting your vision is, but it's only sustained through the way you communicate it, celebrate it, and live it every day. People need to understand your vision, be reminded of it, and see how you role model the vision to remain personally invested in it. But, perhaps most importantly, they need to understand the context and its overall intention. They need to understand the Why. Why are we going there?

The Why is your mission, and it is the mission that motivates your team and gives people a sense of purpose. It communicates why you exist and why others should join with you on your journey. Your mission statement communicates your purpose, and it must be enduring, clear, concise, credible, and compelling.

One example of a great mission statement comes from the International Federation of the Red Cross and Red Crescent Societies, "To protect the lives and dignity of victims of armed conflict and violence and to provide them with assistance." This statement is clear and compelling to mobilize millions of volunteers working on hundreds of projects around the world to work toward a common purpose, a common vision. Another example is the Lion's Club, the world's largest service club, which has just a two-word mission statement: "We Serve." This statement clearly provides their over 1.4 million members from around the world, from different cultures and speaking many languages, the reason why they all do what they do. It is a common denominator that drives everyone, no matter their job or focus or location, to execute the same vision.

Your communication of the vision needs to be compelling, catchy, clear, and constant. A compelling message helps create ongoing buy-in from your team. It also helps them understand the benefits of living the vision, both to themselves and to others, to personally invest in the work that will be necessary to achieve it. A catchy message makes the vision memorable; it sticks in people's minds and cuts through distractions to help your team remember what the vision is in everything they do. If it's a clear message, the team knows exactly what it means and can repeat the message exactly as it is meant to be communicated at any given time.

In communication, repetition creates results. This is why you must constantly be communicating the vision, repeating it over and over again. Bring it to life in your key presentations and team meetings. But you cannot just communicate the vision through speaking and writing. It requires action. Leaders should continually model behaviors they expect from their team members in a way that focuses all minds on the important longer-term goal.

> Can your team members repeat your vision to others with clarity and passion?

Strategic Thinking

When a financial news magazine asked executives what makes the world's most respected companies truly great, the top factor they named was having a sound business strategy. Although great strategic thinking may be among the rarest of executive skills, it is certainly one of the most important.

Your strategy defines how you will achieve your vision based on a number of internal and external factors. Vision is the search for meaning. Strategy is the route that we take to get there. It is simply the search for advantage, and it also ensures you are planning for potential issues in your market. Both of these things factor heavily into our strategic thinking because the strategy can never be done in the absence of destination, and the destination cannot be reached without a clear route.

Strategic thinking can be developed by constructing "memories of the future." When you think back to one of your fondest past memories, what comes to your mind? You may vividly see people with whom you have shared a specific memory; see your surroundings; and sense the sights, sounds, and smells that were around you at that time. Do you recall how you *felt* during this memory? That is exactly the clarity you need to create your memory of the future. What is it that you see, hear, experience, and feel? Make your vision as clear as though it has happened to you already, and then you can start constructing the route—the strategy—that will take you there. This route should be a 2- to 3-year trip, and you must be able to measure your mileage.

Overconfidence, under-optimism, confirmation bias, and following the herd constitute four strategic pitfalls. Leaders may become so *overconfident* in their success that they ignore or neglect to see new information. However, becoming *under-optimistic* or overly pessimistic about their abilities to deliver, or their team's ability to implement new initiatives, can lead managers to focus on how to minimize losses and avoid making mistakes. They're then less likely to take the risks that an organization may need to change and grow.

Confirmation bias is a very common stumbling block in strategic thinking. It's likely to occur when you become so overly confident that you are correct about the future that you will not listen to, or may discourage, contrary points of view. When you are so convinced that your way is right, you actually look for information that proves you right at two to three times the rate of looking for information that says you are wrong. When leaders get information that says they are wrong or biased to the point of opposing any other options, they find ways to discount differing ideas. Confirmation bias keeps you from being open-minded about the data that you see and the ways that you think.

The fourth pitfall is to get caught up in *following the herd* rather than following your own strategic thinking. Herd mentality in the private sector, public sector, and nongovernmental organizations describes how leaders are influenced by industry rivals or pervasive trends to do the same thing as others. Recall that strategic thinking is about finding a competitive advantage to achieve your vision. Although knowing what the herd is doing and where it is going will help clarify common practices, following the herd will not always lead you to greatness.

Being a great strategic thinker does not mean being able to do it all alone. In fact, it is the opposite. You must always find ways to **bring in different views and perspectives about your business to inform your thinking**. Your direct reports and external advisers can help you identify, provided that you are neither overconfident nor under-confident, that your ideas and assumptions are free from confirmation bias, or that you are willing to walk away from the herd in your industry.

Depending on the size of your advisory group, you may want to divide it into subgroups and have group members investigate each one of the strategic thinking pitfalls. Task one of the subgroups to show evidence of overconfidence in your strategic plan. Ask the next to find evidence that your team may be unnecessarily pessimistic. Two other subgroups could address whether your team appears to have confirmation bias and whether your strategic choices put you in the herd.

You can also run a scenarios exercise with your leadership team. Create as many different scenarios as you and your team can think of, and then rank each one in terms of how the scenario leverages your strengths, creates greater competitive advantage, and helps mitigate threats in your market. If you have a large leadership team, you may want to divide it into smaller teams and then have each team present their scenario to the full group. The group can then rank each scenario and discuss its pitfalls.

Once all of this valuable prework is completed, the probability that the team will choose the best strategic direction increases. Leadership should then turn its focus to developing and selecting key initiatives to implement over the coming year or years to achieve the strategy. Involve other key managers and supervisors in the initiative development process. Once advised, prioritize the key initiatives, first by year and then by quarter. Priorities will steer you toward an achievable tactical plan.

Do you have a group of advisers that can provide different perspectives in your strategic thinking?

Plans and Prioritizes

An aspiring young manager in a small U.S.-based medical supply organization found out the hard way how vision and strategy without a plan leads to burnout and frustration. He went to work for the organization largely because he felt connected to the energy of the chief executive officer (CEO) who was innovative, energetic, and full of great ideas. The young man felt compelled to work under him as a role model and a mentor. He was initially ecstatic to land the job, and the first year seemed to offer him the chance to participate in exciting growth. The manager loved getting to know the industry and working with his colleagues.

He believed in the CEO's vision and the mission of the organization and truly felt as though he was going to make an impact.

But, as the first year turned to the second, the manager began to feel the wear of misused time and unfocused energy. The CEO continually came up with great new ideas—ideas that never left the conference room. Due to a lack of structure, focus, and follow-through, the CEO would simply float the idea without assigning responsibility or structure to anyone. As a result of misdirected goals, this young man and the rest of the team became overextended and frustrated. They moved numbly from one idea of the week to the next, never truly completing a project or celebrating *a win*. **Teams need structure and a plan to execute the vision.** They need to achieve closure and key wins related to the work, which they are pouring their energy and expertise into accomplishing, on a daily basis.

An organization can have a great vision, mission, and strategy, but if leaders do not have specific, measurable plans and priorities to support them, teams will not be able to execute the vision. Normally, the first year of the strategy becomes the framework for the annual plan for organizations. The annual plan involves more detail and specifics for the year, and it cascades and links to individual performance goals.

The annual plan may start with top-down guidance from the CEO, working with his or her senior staff to create key organizational goals and assumptions for the year. Each key goal must have a tangible metric and a team member assigned to own the goal.

Depending on the size and complexity of your organization, an annual plan assumption document may be sent to all the functional heads, allowing them to create an organic, bottom-up functional plan and to ensure they can meet the key annual targets—such as the sales goal, production goal, expense reduction, and inflation assumptions—or explain why they cannot meet these goals. The plans are synchronized, and a financial plan is completed. Once the annual plan (including the financial plan) is completed, the functional heads begin to cascade the department and functional targets and goals to their staff, and individual performance plans are completed, ensuring adequate coverage and measurement of each goal. At this level, department heads are charged with delegating the targets and empowering their teams to achieve organizational goals, discussed in greater detail in Chapter 6.

Monitoring the plans and priorities is also a critical element to ensure proper execution of the plans. Prioritize your annual initiatives and sequence them by quarter based on their importance to ensure that you have adequate resources and capacity for achieving the initiatives along with other day-to-day activities. Ensure that you have one owner for each key initiative, and that the owner is responsible for monitoring the initiative, reporting on its status on a periodic basis, and for the overall completion and success of the project. During monthly staff meetings, review financials and ensure that you are tracking on your annual plan initiatives.

- **The Why: Mission**
  Your Fundamental Purpose. Why you exist. Enduring and credible.

- **The What: Vision**
  Your Tangible Intention. An attractive, measurable description of the long-term (10 years) future for your organization.

- **The Strategy**
  Mid-term (3 years) management direction and outcomes that will support the vision.

- **The Prioritization**
  Prioritizing and sequencing the key initiatives by year, and then within quarter. Assigning a point person for each to lead and track progress.

- **The Plans**
  Specific programs and plans that support the strategies and will achieve measurable targets in the next year.

- **The Tracking & Alignment**
  Monthly tracking of all key initiatives and alignment of staff performance plans and related bonus and incentives.

The Why: Purpose

The What: Vision

Growth Strategy

External
(opportunities
& threats)

Business Definition
Markets
Customers
Services
Geography

Internal
(strengths &
weaknesses)

Prioritization

Annual Plan

Dashboard

Performance
Plans

Bonus/
Incentives

Figure 5.1 Translating Vision into Action.

You must ensure that you are monitoring and discussing how you will achieve the plan and what mitigation actions must be implemented to hit the annual plan targets.

How often do you monitor your plans and key initiatives?

Planning can often be complicated by far-reaching details and variables. The planning process can also be as simple as following sequential steps. For example, using the *Seven Steps of Effective Planning* learned in his leadership training, Jürgen, the director of customer management at an industrial equipment sales and rental organization in the heart of Germany, decided to involve the organization's leadership team to improve the repeat client rate, a responsibility that he owned. Jürgen took that goal and broke it down into a plan for his department.

---

7 Steps of Effective Planning

Step 1: Gather the Facts

Step 2: Set the Goal

Step 3: How to Achieve the Goal

Step 4: Who Will Implement the Actions?

Step 5: When Will the Objective Be Implemented?

Step 6: Plan to Implement the Plan

Step 7: Follow-Up and Follow-Through

---

1. Gather the Facts

   Every good plan needs to take the full picture into account. For this, the plan manager initially needs to take the time to gather all the facts that may be relevant to executing the plan. Jürgen knew that they already had a decent base of satisfied customers, but he had learned from his leadership development training that a satisfied customer is not enough. He needed to develop loyal brand ambassadors, and for that they needed to not just meet but exceed customer expectations.

2. Set the Goal

   Setting goals is how teams get the right things done well and on time. Tracking goals helps teams know when they have finished a task, project, or initiative and can count their work as complete. Specific goals also are the measuring stick by which teams and managers can determine how well they have completed their assignments. Jürgen and the rest of the leadership team decided to set a benchmark of increasing repeat customer sales by 20 percent and referral sales from customers by 15 percent. How they would achieve those goals would be up to Jürgen and his department.

3. How to Achieve the Goal

To meet these aggressive goals, Jürgen and his team developed new ideas and approaches to their customer experience. Applying another technique that he had learned from his leadership training, Jürgen gathered his team and facilitated a $\frac{1}{3} + 1$ Method meeting (refer to Chapter 3 for $\frac{1}{3} + 1$ Method) lasting 45 minutes to identify potential Coffee Stains in the business and to brainstorm innovative ways to fix those Coffee Stains. Drawing on what they knew other organizations were doing to engage customers, Jürgen and his team used the $\frac{1}{3} + 1$ Method to identify the top three ideas they could implement over the next 12 months that they believed would help them exceed customer expectations to improve brand loyalty and engagement.

4. Who Will Implement the Actions?

A good plan includes identifying who does what so tasks do not go undone and work is not duplicated. One of the initiatives that Jürgen's team decided to implement was a *Full Circle of Service* program. Among other things, this would include each client having one account person who would stay connected with the client throughout the customer cycle, from the signing of the contract to following up after delivery and then throughout a new ongoing outreach campaign process. Several employees on Jürgen's team volunteered to create the new processes and then train others on the team and throughout the organization.

5. When Will the Objective Be Implemented?

A timetable for implementation was needed for this plan to be successfully executed. Jürgen's team needed to meet the annual goal by the end of the year—in 12 months—for their annual review. They began on the new processes right away by setting milestone goals to prepare for beta testing in 1 month and then ready for organization-wide rollout in 2 months. They planned on having the customer management department fully trained on the new process by the time the full rollout was ready to go, and then have the rest of the organization trained on the process within 4 months.

6. Plan to Implement the Plan

It often happens that goals and benchmarks are discussed and agreed upon, even when a formal plan has not been created. There are a variety of ways, tools, and applications that a manager can use to create a plan. The important thing is to ensure there is a plan, and that the plan has been properly communicated and is being followed by the project team. With a plan in place and full support of the rest of the leadership team, Jürgen was able to lay out each step, check-in dates, and expectations so team members knew what they were accountable to do.

7. Follow-Up and Follow-Through

Even the best plans can fail with lack of follow-through. Leaders who are less effective may create workable project plans and yet fail to effectively communicate the plans to their teams. Always communicate and then follow up and follow through on the actions outlined in the plan. To create a sense of responsibility and accountability in the team, launch each plan together with the respective team members and clarify and ensure commitment to the follow-up and check-in procedures for the project. This is the step where many initiatives fail. They launch the plan, but lose the discipline of a structured follow-up process through project completion.

Managing your team's time is perhaps one of the most difficult aspects of effective planning and prioritization. In today's fast-paced, interconnected business environment, needs and requests from other departments, clients, vendors, and a host of stakeholders threaten to take your focus off your goals. **Develop your ability to manage your team's time against the various requests and priorities that arise,** assessing whether they are aligned with the goals of the department and the organization, and then be able to tell someone "no" when it does not align. Many organizations, teams, and leaders struggle with this issue because it is easy to become distracted from what is most important in complex projects and long-term goals, especially when the context can become diluted by time and distance. However, having an appropriate sense of what is most important to the success of the team and the organization, as well as the ability to effectively manage organizational resources (including staff time) amid a barrage of needs is one of the most important and valuable leadership skills.

Your vision is what drives the actions of your team, and although internal and external factors may force you to adjust your strategy and plans, the mission should remain unchanged. Define a clear, compelling vision that you and your team can enthusiastically support. Then communicate it and continuously demonstrate your own commitment to the vision. Think strategically about the factors that drive your organization or team and develop a strategic plan that is realistically optimistic, unbiased, and influenced by multiple perspectives. The achievement of your strategy will be determined by how well you implement and monitor your annual plans and key initiatives.

Core Competency: Executes Vision

Considers a broad range of internal and external factors when creating strategies and implementing plans. Translates business vision and strategy into plans and sequenced priorities to best deliver results and leverage resources.

Competency Skills

- **Defines and Communicates Vision:** Communicates a compelling picture of the future that connects and motivates others to action
- **Strategic Thinking:** Sees the big picture of future possibility and creates strategic connections leading to competitive advantage
- **Plans and Prioritizes:** Formulates objectives and priorities, implements and monitors plans in alignment with the long-term strategy of the organization

Executes Vision Assessment Questions

1. Can your team members repeat your vision to others with clarity and passion?
2. Do you have a group of advisers that can provide different perspectives in your strategic thinking?
3. How often do you monitor your plans and key initiatives?

The Leader's Toolkit

To get your team thinking about vision and communicating a compelling picture of the future, facilitate the following exercise:

1. Assign small groups (no more than six members to each group) and have each group select a facilitator.
2. Task each group to develop an aspirational headline and visual cover story about your organization ten years in the future.
3. Allow for a few minutes of individual thinking time, and then the group facilitator selects a person to start the story.
4. The story continues to build as it moves around the group and each member adds specifics to the story.

Once this warm-up exercise is complete, each group completes a large poster to visually represent the story. This can be done using flipcharts, whiteboards, or poster board. Each group member adds key elements to the poster (e.g., quotes, images, facts).

1. Once complete, the groups review their vision storyboard and create a headline that they write on the top of their poster.
2. Each group presents to the large group, and the other groups provide comments on what they like about each of the presentations.

CHAPTER

6

Encourages Excellence

est known for painting *Mona Lisa* and *The Last Supper*, Leonardo da Vinci
began his vocation as an apprentice. Classical European artists collectively
produced much of the world's most renowned paintings, and to work as an
apprentice of a master painter was considered the path to excellence. In the
workshop of the Italian master artist, Andrea del Verrocchio, Da Vinci learned
a range of technical skills that many today would not consider part of becoming a
painter, including drafting, chemistry, metallurgy, plaster casting, mechanics, and
carpentry—along with the artistic skills of drawing, sculpting, and painting. The
great masters trained their apprentices to be knowledgeable in a variety of topics
and skills not just by teaching but by doing.

Da Vinci was one of the pupils of Verrocchio. There were others, and we can
learn from the way the master trained. The ways of developing young artists had
been and was still at the time institutionalized in European society. In a master's
workshop, the junior budding artists like Da Vinci were schooled in every step of
the process, such as preparing pigments and canvases.

There is a lesson for business leaders in the way that classical artists developed
the next generation of excellent painters. Although apprenticed painters studied
the style and works of their masters, they also contributed to production. In the
Renaissance era, when Verrocchio and Da Vinci both lived, masterpieces were
often painted collaboratively. Da Vinci's significant contributions on Verrocchio's
team started with an angel depicted by Da Vinci in Verrocchio's famous *Baptism of
Christ* painting. The angel was a small element painted on the lower left corner of
Verrocchio's large project, and it was one less thing that Verrocchio had to
accomplish himself. In fact, it is known that much of the painting being produced
by Verrocchio's workshop was actually done by his artists, leaving Verrocchio

himself to pursue his first passion—sculpting—because he could simply direct his artists and apprentices, correcting their work and administering final touches.

In the context of modern business, effective leaders do a similar thing. They delegate and empower and, at the same time, coach, encourage, and recognize the contributions of others. The work accomplished in most organizations depends on the collaboration of teams. The greatest organizational achievements happen as a result of leaders who encourage excellence.

Think of yourself as the master painter. Is there budding talent within your team that needs to be cultivated? Once you see the relationship between higher productivity and your ability to delegate, empower, coach, encourage, reward, and recognize, you are more likely to be ready to paint your masterpiece.

Delegation and Empowerment

Delegating responsibility and empowering individuals on your team encourages excellence by motivating everyone to personally invest in achieving common goals. How do you talk about goals with your team? Do you simply monitor progress against these goals or do you link them to the overall purpose of the organization?

Motivation is a huge element to delegation and empowerment. You have likely experienced situations when you have delegated a responsibility or task to someone who was not motivated to accept it. The results of this are always going to be poor. Some managers feel that employees should just be grateful to have a job and that alone should motivate them to show up to work with passion and commitment. **But people do things for their reasons, not your reasons**.

Employees are a lot like customers. Customers have demands and expectations of your organization. If you deliver on those, they will be highly satisfied; they will become loyal; and they will become advocates for your brand. In this way, employees and customers are the same. They have certain expectations, like highly satisfying work. If you can find a way to create a highly satisfying work environment, you will inspire the passion and commitment necessary for encouraging a team to deliver excellence.

Structuring Excellence

Whatever your motives are, they are your wants. You may be highly motivated and passionate about your job because you believe that your work is meaningful and will help you achieve your personal goals. Your employees are wired similarly and will own and achieve the goals of your team when their work is aligned with their personal motivators. The key is that their motivators may be different than yours. Until you know what their specific motivations are, it is very hard to motivate anybody.

Surprisingly, many managers overlook the simple yet fundamental leadership practice of asking and listening. Simply ask each of your direct reports what motivates him or her, and then actually listen to understand. Schedule a 30-minute one-on-one meeting and have your employee prepare for the meeting by answering this question: What motivates you and why? Be inquisitive and ask questions to ensure that you understand the employee's personal motivations. Planned one-on-one conversations about the specific things that drive employees to achieve can also help the members of your team to better understand their own motivators.

For example, employees may say that they are motivated by money, but what is it about money that motivates them? Do they want money to pay for their children to attend a good school? Perhaps they work to afford a lifestyle, an opportunity to travel, or another desire. Dig deeper and try to understand where the motivation is coming from to learn more about the whole person.

Your greater understanding will affect the way that you lead and motivate every individual. A person who is motivated by money for material things may be fine with working more hours to reach a goal, and an additional financial bonus or incentive is a great motivator for that person. Others may want additional time off as an incentive for their achievement and extra efforts. And some individuals are motivated by their personal achievement and development and want new challenges that will help them grow.

Your attitude toward your employees will determine their attitude toward you. If it is obvious that you care and are interested in them, they will be more likely to care about and be interested in what is important to you and the organization. As you understand the key motivators of the individuals on your team, you are better equipped to lead the team, personalize the goals, and clearly communicate your expectations.

Do you understand what motivates each one of your team members?

Communicating expectations is the key to delegation and empowerment success. Yet, many managers fail to take the time upfront to communicate their expectations and align with their team. Employees are not mind readers, and you cannot expect your team to perform the way you want them to unless you first let them know what you expect. Clearly **communicate your expectations to your team and set your standards for excellence**. This includes defining what great looks like to your team and involving them in developing this definition. Generally, performance can be defined as

- **Above Target:** This is your *great* performance metric; the employee consistently exceeds expectations beyond the day-to-day role. This metric is extremely difficult to achieve.
- **On Target:** This is your *good* performance metric; the employee consistently is hitting targets, adding value to the project and organization, and deserving of recognition.
- **Below Target:** This is your *improvement required* performance metric for an employee who is unsuccessful in reaching his or her responsibility targets.

Ensuring clarity of the direction and scope of work is important. Investigate your employees' understanding of expectations and progress toward their goals in your one-on-one meetings to make sure that their understanding of the goals and expectations of a delegated responsibility is aligned with your expectations.

The next step is to further structure your expectations by clarifying roles and individual goals. All team members should understand what they and everyone else are responsible for, and how they all work together as a team. Goals are inspired by your vision and then expressed in specific language, measureable deliverables, and timelines. Tracking goals makes people accountable for the responsibilities that have been delegated to them. It provides a road map to their destination. If you communicate your expectations for excellence and establish clear goals, then you have provided the basis for high performance by your team.

Communicating Excellence

Communication and clarity is an ongoing process to ensure ongoing engagement and excellence. A great way to improve team communication is to huddle with your team on a regular basis. This means getting everybody on the team involved. This does not necessarily need to be a sit-down meeting; it can be a quick stand-up huddle to briefly share information to align the team. This sort of open and regular communication is crucial if you expect your team to be engaged. By huddling up regularly, people are reminded why they are there, what they are working toward, and why it is important. This reminder helps make them feel their importance and reasserts the ways they may contribute to the bigger picture. Group communication encourages excellence toward the common purpose that everyone on the team is working to achieve.

Engaging Excellence

Engage everyone in these meetings by asking questions. Ask for suggestions. After the team has shared information and updated one another on current projects or tasks, ask for opinions and suggestions. Set the table for employee-generated action plans, not directives that come down from above. Those directives may be necessary occasionally, but the **most passionately embraced action plans will be the ones that people create themselves or together as a team**.

Even if you have realized the best solution or action before meeting with your team, hold your own thoughts and engage your team in the discussion. People are smart. They will frequently come to the same conclusions you had, and may have additional perspectives or solutions that had not occurred to you. You cannot lose by asking your team members their opinion; rather, you will see more ownership of plans and solutions when they are included in influencing the direction.

Sharing information with your team and engaging them in action plans sets the groundwork for creating a climate of empowered excellence. Through these group dynamics, excellence will then become the norm in your team. Because those team members who are engaged outnumber those who are not, they create the group norm that makes it possible for someone who is not engaged or who does not care about the work to reorient or recommit.

Disengagement and negativity will not normally be tolerated by peers on a team that has established excellence as a norm. Be mindful, however, that the power of group dynamics can also work against you. Strong leaders cultivate the social climate on the team, but group dynamics will always work to create a climate when this kind of leadership is missing.

Managers who neglect their responsibilities to share information or set clear goals and expectations lose positive control of their team. Instead, that control is gained by others within the team who will often cultivate the climate of negativity and complacency rather than excellence and engagement. In this environment, the danger exists that team members will cultivate the mindset that they are mere pawns in a game with nothing to gain from raising the bar of excellence. They lower the bar of excellence, and they persecute those team members who outperform. So be aware that group dynamics can be used as either a force for good or bad in cultivating your team.

A volunteer Little League soccer coach did not know much about soccer, but he understood the importance of group dynamics and cultivating a climate of excellence and engagement. When the kids on the team came to practice, the first thing they would do was sit down in a circle and talk. They would talk as teammates—as people—and they would talk about what they did since the last practice, and about friends and pets and hobbies and things that interested them. After roughly 5 minutes, the coach would stop them and redirect them to talk about what they were going to do in practice that day. He used these techniques of sharing information and engaging everyone in conversation to build respect for one another.

This was one of the most cooperative teams in the league. Nobody was grasping to be the super star. They were unselfish, cooperative players. The coach could influence their attitudes and their environment to create this climate of cooperation and respect. On some of the other teams, when things went badly, they were more likely to start blaming each other and to lose their tempers.

Delegating Excellence

Think about yourself as the team creator and help your team get to know and understand one another. Build a communicative team so that when someone achieves, the rest of the team feels like it is their shared success because they are invested in the success and welfare of each other. Perhaps the best way to engage your team is to empower them and delegate greater responsibility. It can be exciting to be entrusted with a position of responsibility, so if something makes you feel a sense of self-worth, give that self-worth to others on your team.

Find areas where you can give people the responsibility and, importantly, the authority to get things done. Have you ever heard from your team that they cannot finish their work because they are waiting for you? They are waiting for you to look at their work or approve it? That may be a prime example of areas that you should consider letting go. Empower and, if necessary, train them, coach them, encourage them, and reward them. Otherwise, they will continue without authority and you may be the cog in your own wheel.

Take a minute to do a mental exercise. Imagine you have been given a special assignment that will require you to be out of the office for the next 3 months. During those 3 months, all of your work still has to get done, but you are not allowed to hire anybody new. Before the special assignment begins, you have 30 days to figure out how you will redistribute your work. Pick up your pen, and for a few seconds think about to whom you would start delegating more responsibility. Write down one to three things that you would start delegating. The reality is that a leader cannot perpetually do everything that needs to get done. You need others who are empowered to complete critical tasks, and you need backup.

Do you clearly delegate responsibility and authority?

This exercise was a reality for Lucas, a supervisor in a construction and public works organization based in France, who fell and was seriously injured while skiing with his family in the Swiss Alps during his winter holiday. Suddenly unable to assume his normal functions in the workplace for several months, he had no alternative than to delegate the bulk of his responsibilities to two of his foremen, Lorenzo and Noam. Lucas knew that both foreman had recently completed leadership training and were excited to take on the additional responsibility, which they had been working toward being able to take on in the event of any organizational changes.

Knowing that the foremen would still have to complete their own duties while taking on his, Lucas divided his responsibilities between the two to help alleviate the burden of the extra work. He began by creating a list of all the projects he was supervising, complete with a high-level list of all his responsibilities within each project, such as managing project staff and subcontractors, project management, code compliance and enforcement, health and safety regulation compliance, and customer service and satisfaction. He then detailed the smaller tasks that contributed to completing those responsibilities—daily work site checkups; writing up noncompliance; attending daily, weekly, and monthly client update calls; working with the sales and accounts team to quote new projects; and so on.

Lucas then created a three-column document, which he labeled with each of their names—leaving one column for himself and the responsibilities he would keep and be able to accomplish despite his reduced time and mobility constraints. Doing his best to divide the workload evenly, Lucas assigned his ongoing projects between the two foremen based on size and complexity of each project. Lucas decided to keep responsibilities associated with quoting new projects and handling any high-profile compliance issues or customer complaints that might come up.

With his plan set up, Lucas called a meeting with Lorenzo and Noam to discuss the specifics of his plan and answer any of their questions. With their new responsibilities and an eagerness to apply their recently developed leadership skills, Lorenzo and Noam demonstrated an increased capacity to lead.

Together, they tackled their new challenges. They encouraged each other to refer back to their leadership class materials and apply them to address the field of new issues that were part of the duties delegated by Lucas. Working together to apply the change management, customer service, communication, and time-management tools they had practiced in their leadership classes, they broadened their experience leading teams and projects to improve productivity, quality assurance, and customer satisfaction.

On different occasions, both Lorenzo and Noam repeatedly used a process for dealing with dissatisfied customers that they had learned. By delegating, Lucas had elevated the value of two leadership-ready members of his team; as a result of empowering Lorenzo and Noam, the company benefited from the new perspectives and new leadership methods. They consistently communicated the *Afters* of every project and task assigned to their teams, a simple communication innovation that helped slash rework and improve project productivity so much that most of their projects were running on or ahead of schedule. Customer complaints were also reduced. They worked hard to develop the trust and respect they needed from their teams to effectively manage the changes they were making, and they expanded their roles to become trusted leaders of people who had previously been their peers.

Several months later, when Lucas returned to his regular work schedule, he was delighted to find that Lorenzo and Noam had not only been able to properly conduct business in his absence but that they had improved significant aspects of daily operations. Construction teams were operating at a high level of productivity and conflicts with subcontractors and regulators had decreased.

Lucas recognized Lorenzo and Noam publicly at the next company meeting for their success in taking on and excelling in their extra responsibilities. He also rewarded their achievement with a sizable bonus and expressed his gratitude with gift cards to take their spouses to dine at a nice restaurant.

Lorenzo and Noam were happy to have been able to apply their leadership skills to help the organization succeed during a time of unforeseen need, as well as prove their ability to take on additional responsibilities within the organization. Lucas increasingly included them in asking for their advice and opinions on managing projects and dealing with conflicts as they arose. They trained others in the organization on the skills they had applied, and innovations they started were adopted throughout the organization. Not surprisingly, both were soon promoted to do even more for the company.

Empowering Excellence

When you have an empowered workforce, and everybody is genuinely engaged and giving 100 percent of his or her capacity, you will be able to pursue more strategic organizational priorities. You may also be able to decrease the amount of time you spend at the office each week and instead begin to focus on building or extending your professional network.

What would you have to give up to get a totally inspired, totally engaged workforce? Few leaders think about delegation in this way, because they have a difficult time giving up control to gain the benefits of delegation and empowerment. Leaders want their teams to be autonomous, empowered, and excellent; yet, teams are rarely given the space to be able to do so.

Delegating responsibility without giving up control and assigning authority will only result in undermining that which you are trying to achieve. Focus on the outcomes of the goal and allow your employees to figure out how they will accomplish it. And then make sure you are following up and helping them with obstacles that may occur. You must be willing and able to give up control to gain the benefits.

However, what do your employees gain from a totally empowered, inspired, and engaged workforce? And what do they have to give up to get that? They gain more opportunity, perhaps more recognition for their work. They get a higher level of responsibility and maybe advances in their careers. But, they also must let go of some things to achieve this. They must give up the feeling of being safe, or of always falling back on the decisions of others. They must give up the ability to complain about things, and they must give up the not-my-fault attitude.

These questions illustrate the fundamental issue of delegation and empowering employees. It is an issue of control versus initiative. Leaders claim that they would give employees more control if they show more initiative; employees reply that they would show more initiative if they had more control. It is a chicken or egg paradox. It is a balancing act in which leaders need to find a counterbalance to cede more control to stimulate more initiative, and there are ways to improve this counterbalance to make delegation and empowerment work for everyone.

First, you need trust. If you damage trust, the control versus initiative balance will erode. **People are far less likely to take extra initiative if they cannot trust their leaders.** Leaders who cannot trust their followers are far less likely to cede control. Both leaders and employees must be trustworthy, and to achieve this you must be authentic and you must have integrity because once trust is broken it is extremely difficult to repair.

Second, you need clear and open communication. Research has shown that the two things that derail most leaders at some point in their careers are lack of trust and poor communication. When leaders think of poor communication, they often think of it in terms of not enough communication. More often, it is a case of the quality and relevance of what is being communicated. You might be feeling like you are repeating yourself or are overcommunicating. Managers tend to get frustrated when communication efforts do not have a positive effect on the team. But the real question to ask yourself, and your team, is whether you are communicating the right information and the most relevant information.

Next, recognizing and rewarding the right people for their achievements will help this control versus initiative balance. This chapter later addresses rewards and recognition but emphasizes here that rewards and recognition are essential tools in your leadership toolkit—and one of the primary ways to keep people engaged in excellence when you are delegating responsibility.

Perhaps most importantly, do not make the mistake of taking credit for other people's work. It is easily the most damaging thing that you can do as a leader. **Taking credit for your team's work will immediately negate any trust and credibility you may have built** with your team, and you will lose the ability to communicate effectively with them or engage them toward a shared goal.

The last way to improve the control versus initiative balance in your organization or team is to ask people for ideas and then try them out. That is not to say that every idea that comes across your desk is pure gold or that you should embrace every one. There is clearly a balance that needs to be struck. But for those ideas that are legitimately good ideas, you need to give your team the opportunity and the space to try them out. Will they always be successful? No. But, sometimes they will. And if you have a competent, passionately engaged, and motivated team, chances are good that they will have some great ideas that can truly make an impact for the organization. When you ask for ideas, but then never try any of them out, the only thing you will get is undermotivation.

Coaching and Encouraging

Excellence is encouraged most effectively, and perhaps most rewardingly, when a leader takes the role of the coach. This is what leadership is all about. You are preparing the next generation of great leaders, and this is perhaps the most important role you play in your organization. Your ability to coach and encourage excellence in your team has a multiplier effect toward the success of your organization. When you are coaching, you are developing. You are helping others become better contributors, leaders, better thinkers, and better decision makers.

Coaching is a time when you role model for your team members. Keep in mind that you do not want to create a perfect-model persona that seems so flawless that your employee sees your level of success as unattainable. Success is never a straight line, so talk about your failures and the lessons that you learned from those failures as well as your successes.

Make sure your team members understand that it is okay to make mistakes as long as they take responsibility for those mistakes and learn from them. One suggestion is to **keep a page of the 10 worst mistakes you have made and what you have learned from them**. Include at least one mistake that is fairly recent so as not to imply that all of your mistakes were a long time ago and that you are now perfect. If you can show that you can make a mistake, bounce back from it, and learn from that experience, they will be more comfortable in the knowledge that they can do the same. Mistakes engender energy and wisdom.

You do not want your people leaving a coaching session thinking, "I am so impressed with my coach." You want them leaving thinking, "I am impressed with what I am able to do as a result of having been coached."

Great coaching requires clear expectations, boundaries, and goals that are consistently reinforced. Performance goals and one-on-one reviews allow managers and employees to work together to clarify goals and then track how they are performing against those goals throughout the year. Begin each calendar year with the creation of a performance plan. This performance plan should detail the employee's key accomplishments for the coming year, which are written in the form of goals and must align with the goals and the vision of the organization.

A-SMART Goals

Aligned—consistent with overall organization's goals

Specific—defines a precise target

Measurable—includes a benchmark for determining success (quantity, speed, cost, quality)

Action oriented—describes what needs to be done

Realistic—the objective is achievable

Time-Bound—includes a date by which success will be achieved

Include details that specify exactly what goal achievement looks like and how it will be measured in your team's performance plans. Then meet one-on-one with your direct reports monthly to discuss how they are tracking against their goals, what other projects and priorities have come up that may require a change in their goals, and how they are developing overall. This is an important time to provide your clear feedback and discuss what corrections or improvements should be made to ensure that your employees perform at a high standard and develop personally as well as professionally. Also use this time to give your employees a chance to coach up and provide feedback to you. Ask what they think you could be doing to improve as their manager, leader, and coach. **Ask them, "What do you need from me?" and "How can I best help you?"**

Formal midyear and end-of-year reviews normally take place around June and December. First, get your team members to rate themselves on how they are tracking against their goals formally by using your organization's rating scale. For example, performance plans can be rated on the same Below-Target, On-Target, and Above-Target rating system described previously, and they should include space for employees to include notes and comments on why they assessed themselves at that rating. Review self-assessments carefully and then provide your own assessment on the performance plan, including your detailed notes.

If your employee's self-rating is significantly different from how you would rate the performance, then who owns that miscommunication? This is a clear indicator that you have not adequately provided feedback along the way to ensure clarity of expectations and performance standards. The monthly one-on-ones, the midyear review, and the end-of-year review are all important times to provide clear feedback to your employees. Do not wait until the formal midyear or annual review to provide feedback. Many organizations are moving away from annual reviews and replacing with frequent, informal check-ins. Both approaches work, with your goal of helping your employees be successful along the way. There should be *no* surprises come evaluation time. Employees should always know how they are performing.

Great coaches balance positive reinforcement and encouragement with clear and honest feedback. They view feedback as an opportunity for improvement, and they can convey that to their employees as well. Also use this time to ask questions that encourage your employees to develop themselves. Helping your employees view feedback as a gift is key to your employee's continued development.

As a leader, you are less known by what you say. You are more known by the questions you consistently ask.

> How often do your employees receive feedback on what they are doing well and what they need to improve?

Effective coaches understand the power of consistent questions. Regularly set aside time with members of your team and ask them consistent questions. For example, one leader would take a 15-minute walk with each direct report every week. The questions he asked every week were: "What is working?" "What is not working?" "What have you learned?" Because the leader asked that question every week, every week his direct reports came prepared to share something that had worked.

If you want your employee, especially someone you may be coaching, to read more, ask the question, "What have you read this week that brought you the most wisdom and that maybe we could share as part of our discussion?" The first time you ask that, the employee might get caught a little off guard, and might respond with, "Oh, I didn't know I was supposed to read." But if you ask that question in each of your sessions, you will begin to find that the employee is reading more and starting to consciously look for insights and ideas. They will bring information to you that allows you to be impressed with the knowledge and information that they are learning.

Another good question to consistently ask is, "Do you see any red flags on the project you're working on?" Most people who are being developed will not want to admit that there is a problem. But if you let them know that it is okay to talk about red flags early on in your coaching relationship, there is a good chance that you will be able to intervene early when the problem is still manageable.

One chief executive officer (CEO) has a quote on his desk that reads, **"The question is the answer."** If you spend time telling your employees everything instead of listening to what they have learned, you are not developing independent thinkers. You are just transmitting data and information, and little of it may be relevant or retained. Your job is to make sure you do not create dependence but rather foster independence.

Have you created a dependent or independent workforce?

Independence is a key component and indicator to being a successful coach. Not only do you want to develop independent thinkers, but you should be so dedicated and excited about your coaching experiences that you can create coaching alumni that feel proud to have worked with you. Throughout their careers, they will always remember the experiences they had while working for you and being coached by you, so much so that they will become advocates for you and your organization.

Rewards and Recognition

When individuals and teams work above and beyond expectations to achieve great results, celebration and recognition is how great leaders encourage continued commitment to the organization's goals and mission. When your team can step up and make things happen, it is important to recognize the work as a team to encourage further collaboration. Celebration and recognition is how excellence is encouraged over time and how it stays strong even in times of high production volume and stress.

What gets rewarded gets repeated. This statement has become a business maxim, yet managers still often overlook the positive impact of rewarding and recognizing excellence. Studies have shown that only 60 percent of adults in the workplace will agree that personal recognition is important to them and that it works well to help keep them motivated. That means that 40 percent will say they do not really need recognition. They believe they are self-motivated enough to work well without recognition. And yet, 96 percent of the people in that same group responded that, when they receive personal recognition, it definitely inspires and motivates them to do more work.[5] The conclusion is that, although they may not need recognition, recognition does inspire people to do more and better work.

Employees want to feel appreciated. They want to feel valued. It instills a sense of commitment. Often when leaders think of rewarding employees, they think in terms of a bonus, a raise, a promotion, or some kind of gift. Organizations spend billions of dollars a year worldwide on reward programs that, in the long run, do not work. They may work in the short run because people will work hard to win that incentive program, but it will not have the lasting effect of higher productivity and motivation. Some organizations may host events where top performers are recognized and rewarded for their contributions monthly, quarterly, or yearly. The truth is that these events do little to incentivize those who are not top performers to improve. Furthermore, it is highly likely that 90 percent of those top performers would still be top performers without the event. They just have it in them, so to speak—they like recognition, but they do not necessarily need it.

Not every organization has the budget for elaborate, expensive reward programs. The good news is that they really are not needed to reward excellence. In fact, reward and recognition are far more effective when you get into the habit of recognizing in a timely manner the specific actions that deserve praise. **Recognizing *specific* actions is one of the keys to effective recognition.** If you were to just walk around the office, clapping your hands and telling your employees, "Good job." "Good job." "Good job." "Good job," what happens to them after casually, mindlessly hearing "Good job" here and there? They become numb to it, and the hollow statement gradually means less and less the more they hear it.

It is important to note that managers can make the mistake of giving praise in terms of "my staff." They may stand up in front of a group and say, "My staff has had a wonderful year." As if the staff was his or hers. In fact, the person who says "my staff" is looking for credit for himself or herself. What the person is in effect saying is, "Promote me. Give me a bonus; give me a raise, because I somehow got 'my staff' to do a good job this year." The person may not be intentionally devious about it, but he or she is not communicating recognition in an effective way. It does, however, give the impression to the team that their manager does not care and that the manager feels above the team. Do not make this mistake when recognizing your team.

Do a small amount of homework to gather specifics to recognize excellence with impact. Find out what employees did to deserve recognition, how they did it, why they did it, and for whom they did it. Perhaps most importantly, you need to find out how the organization benefited from what they did. It may take a grand total of about 5 minutes to gather the information you need to recognize with lasting impact.

Next, you will need to decide how you will use the information to recognize excellence. Recognition is very powerful when you recognize people publicly. A great way to do this is while opening a team meeting. Never again should any manager or leader begin an employee meeting in any other way than with recognition! Recognition can also be a very powerful tool for team building. You do not need to spend a lot of money to accomplish this. A simple, yet effective recognition party can be hosted in your office for very little money.

A small professional services organization based in the United States did just this using a group recognition party that everyone participated in. After several months of pushing hard and clocking a lot of overtime to get several key initiatives completed, the team was feeling accomplished but a bit burned out. To wrap it up and reignite the passion of working together as a team, the CEO of the organization tasked the office manager, Jenny, to coordinate a fun party and team-building activity. Doing a little bit of research, Jenny decided on a group recognition exercise that would help let everyone on the team recognize each other's contributions and be recognized in turn.

Jenny first blocked out the time on everyone's calendar to hold an office party and then purchased enough large candy bars and a gift card for each person in the office. She then asked the CEO to write general "Thank You!" notes, enough for each person in the office, which she taped to the back of each candy bar, along with a gift card. When the time came for the party to start, she placed the treats in a large bowl in the middle of the common area in the office and invited the team to sit at tables placed in a circle.

The CEO then began the recognition party by reading a selection of client testimonials to remind everyone how their work had affected others in so many ways. Then he explained the rules of the exercise and asked someone to volunteer to go first with the candy bowl. Every employee got a turn to go to the bowl, pick out a large candy bar (with the gift card attached) and decide who they wanted to give it to as an expression of thanks. When each one presented the gift to another, he or she recognized the individual for the work and contributions made. The simple recognition included things that had positively affected someone personally or benefited the team. Then, each person in the group was given a chance to say something nice to recognize that person as well. The person who was recognized, in turn, selected a candy bar and a different person to recognize. Each person on the team received one candy bar, and everyone was recognized.

The impact of the exercise was amazing and truly heartfelt. Each person on the team felt the impact that their efforts and work had had on each other. Sentimental as this exercise can be, leaders should assess the suitability of the exercise for their teams. But whether using this type of activity or something else, an emotional recognition-focused meeting, with or without laughter or tears, can reconnect a team around the mission of the organization and reignite the team's energy to continue to produce excellent work.

Most often, public recognition is the most powerful and impactful way to recognize excellence. However, some people may feel uncomfortable with public recognition, and if you get to know your people you will discover who may feel uncomfortable with public recognition. In those cases, pull them aside prior to the public recognition to forewarn them and help them prepare. Another option is to forgo public recognition altogether with that person and instead use a handwritten note or possibly a gift card. A handwritten note is a simple and effective recognition method that most people appreciate, even those who may also be recognized publicly.

When writing a note, it is important to be specific to show the employee you really understand and truly appreciate his or her efforts. For example:

Dear Yvette,

Your quick response to our client's shipping issue by working on Saturday tells me you're really committed to our values, so thank you! You rushed that shipment so they would receive it on time for their presentation, and it was greatly appreciated. Your excellence delighted our client and ensures that they will continue to order through us in the future. You're a great team player and role model our values!

Sincerely,

Set a goal to write handwritten notes to recognize people on your team each week. If you supervise other managers, encourage each of them to write hand-written thank-you notes to people on their teams on a weekly basis as well. It is a simple activity that takes a very small amount of time. But if you do it consistently, specifically, and authentically, you will start to see improvements in morale and engagement.

What would the benefits of consistent, specific recognition be? There is a well-known quote that states, "People leave bosses, not companies." **Recognition is a simple, effective way to improve morale and lower turnover.** With lower turnover and higher morale, productivity and engagement increase. Good behaviors get duplicated and repeated as employees are recognized by managers. If you can make the small effort to figure out who deserves recognition and why, and then recognize those individuals, others who experience the impact and benefit of it will begin to do the same thing.

Perhaps the most important part of recognition is to start doing it right now. Do not let it lag. Recognition is most effective when used as close to the event as possible. Building a culture of excellence requires more than walking around the office or job site clapping your hands together like a seal and telling everyone he or she is doing a good job.

> How many people did you recognize last week?

The great master painters of the past deliberately created excellence, and their process involved delegating, empowering, coaching, encouraging, rewarding, and recognizing. Today, your canvas is the potential for excellence. Excellence requires sincere passion, and that passion must come from you and permeate down throughout your organization.

Core Competency: Encourages Excellence

Empowers and motivates team members to achieve and creates a feeling of personal investment and desire to excel. Appropriately recognizes the contributions of individuals and teams. Nurtures the development of others through effective coaching and mentoring.

Competency Skills

- **Delegation and Empowerment:** Establishes clear performance goals that encourage others to personally connect to their job
- **Coaching and Encouraging:** Develops others by providing clear feedback on performance and offering positive coaching advice and opportunities to develop skills
- **Rewards and Recognition:** Provides specific, meaningful, and timely recognition to individuals and teams for their results

Encourages Excellence Assessment Questions

1. Do you understand what motivates each one of your team members?
2. Do you clearly delegate responsibility and authority?
3. How often do your employees receive feedback on what they are doing well and what they need to improve?
4. Have you created a dependent or independent workforce?
5. How many people did you recognize last week?

The Leader's Toolkit

1. Order personalized notecards and create a habit of writing short personal notes to your employees to specifically thank them for their hard work and excellence. You may even see your notecards posted in your employees' offices or cubicles. A thank-you note goes a long way toward letting your employees know you appreciate and value them.
2. Set up standard one-on-one sessions with each of your employees. Ensure that you do not cancel or move these sessions and communicate your preparation expectations. Here is a recommended process for your one-on-one sessions:
   a. A general check-in of how they are doing overall
   b. Actions and progress from prior meeting

    c. Key accomplishments

    d. Feedback: First ask for their feedback on how they feel about their progress, what they have learned, and what they would improve to date. Then, provide your feedback and observations with specifics of what they did well and what they need to improve.

    e. Ask, "What do I need to know about?" Here, you are looking for key things that have occurred or may be occurring in the near future.

    f. Ask, "What help do you need from me?"

    g. Decide on action items from current meeting.

Develops Positive Relationships

Peppermint tea evidently provides numerous health benefits, such as reducing pain, resting the mind, relaxing the body, improving digestion, aiding in weight loss, and relieving some of the effects of stomach ulcers. It even cures bad breath, so they say. But although peppermint tea appears to be a kind of panacea for aches and pains, can it also help you develop positive relationships?

Although not literally a leadership tool, a cup of tea might be just what you need to warm up your people skills. After all, your ability to build positive relationships can determine whether others will work with you, buy from you, listen to you, or even respect you. Nelson Mandela used sharing tea in a cordial way to break through tension with a political opponent. In fact, tea has frequently been used in diplomacy.

Diplomacy belongs in business as much as it does in politics. And a cup of peppermint tea may be the thing that disarms tension or infuses good will into business relationships, just as it did for Mandela.

Although drinking this magic herbal drink together can warm relationships, business leaders and managers are much more likely to profit by developing productive habits and skills in networking, collaborating, and also managing conflict. Productive habits lead to positive outcomes, and creating a positive outcome is the objective of positive relationships.

The aim of the leader is building relationships that drive or inspire people to achieve a common goal. To build and maintain positive relationships, leaders must be able to recognize and show respect for other people, ideas, and perspectives even if they do not agree with them or if they may have a different personality or style from others. Leaders must also actively seek to constructively resolve interpersonal disagreement and conflict to keep the team working together and productive. A great leader will be able to nurture relationships both inside and outside of the organization to reach positive results for their connections, organizations, teams, and communities.

Networking

Many people think of networking as a social media connection or an awkward conversation at a conference or event with a stranger who they may never hear from again. When you ask successful leaders what single habit helped them most in their career advancement, the response is overwhelmingly networking. When done correctly, networking creates a foundation of personal and professional contacts that can provide advice, more connections, perspectives, expertise, and experiences to the questions and challenges you or your organization face. In fact, many **executives who maintain strong networks of digital and face-to-face relationships are believed to be up to 30 percent more productive than people who do not leverage their networks.**

Networking is a difficult task for many managers and leaders, but it can be a particularly difficult activity for newer managers who often become managers based on technical knowledge or job-specific ability. They do not fully appreciate the highly relational aspects of becoming a manager, yet they have questions and challenges that they are unprepared to handle in their new leadership roles.

More experienced and senior leaders have built networks through years of experience, although they can also face feelings of being alone at the top if they do not have a network for feedback or advice on issues. To combat this, many executive-level leaders are increasingly joining peer advisory groups in which they can meet with other executives and business leaders to share insights, knowledge, ideas, and contacts.

For newer managers, internal networking is a great place to either start or improve networking skills. As employees move into management positions, they often find that they need to be able to work cross-functionally with other departments more so than before. Reaching out to colleagues within your organization, even if your job does not specifically require you to do so, is how you can improve your ability to ensure your department is effectively working toward big-picture goals.

Great internal networkers understand that connecting with and creating value for others in their organization, not just those within their department, improves the performance of all. **Internal networking is *not* about playing office politics or trying to maneuver for special projects, favors, or promotions.**

Internal networking is best used to improve your knowledge of the organization, to develop relationships across the organization, and possibly to establish one or more mentoring relationships. The outcome could spark a special project recommendation or a cross-functional move, but that should not be the sole intent of your outreach. Be authentic in your intent and curious about the organization. Ask your boss to recommend others in the organization who you should get to know. Reach out and congratulate colleagues who are promoted or who complete an important initiative. Be known as someone who helps others in the organization through sharing knowledge, experience, and access to your network.

Great leaders do not just keep all knowledge and new ideas within their departments. They have a network within the organization that they can tap into when they need to influence or enlist stakeholders in complex projects or initiatives. Some might see this dependence as a weakness, but leaders know it is a strength.

Always be looking for people who can mentor you to help you grow. Also look for people who you can help and mentor. Invest time in others and ensure that others are benefiting from your knowledge and perspective. As you progress in your career and are assigned more complex, cross-functional projects, having well-rounded knowledge and relationships throughout the organization will significantly aid in the success of your projects.

Many organizations around the world have experienced group team-building sessions or workshops that help their teams work toward establishing internal networks. The organizations that are most effective in this are those that take a long-term view of this approach. When a medical product manufacturing organization with several locations throughout Canada initially involved its management team in an interactive leadership development program that was ongoing, instead of the 1-day or weekend training they previously had tried, the team members began to realize the difference almost immediately. The managers not only were learning important new skills individually, but they also were working together—in-person and in cross-functional groups—in a way they had never done before. They realized just how siloed their organization had been, and how those silos had developed a bit of a strategic disadvantage for the organization as a whole.

Through their participation in leadership development, this organization's managers are now speaking the same language and reaching across teams to collaborate and share knowledge, experiences, and perspectives. By building and sustaining those networks, they have been able to open lines of communication and significantly reduce conflicts. They have been able to reduce their weekly multisite conference call meetings from 90 minutes to 30 minutes. The overall impact of their training completely changed the culture of the organization, making it an exciting, inclusive place to work. They have continued to send managers and employees into the same leadership development program while experiencing compounding results in the team's ability to network and collaborate across departments and locations throughout Canada.

Are you known as someone who helps others in the organization?

Your ability as a leader to tap into networks outside of your organization is just as important as those within it. External networking also becomes more critical as you progress in your career and as your responsibilities broaden to become more big-picture and future-oriented. External networking includes attending professional meetings; community events and boards; and establishing and maintaining relationships with friends, neighbors, and family.

Make a habit of having coffee or lunch with at least one new person a month. Professionals can detrimentally excuse themselves from making new contacts because they may not have creatively considered topics or questions that could be discussed during these introductory meetings. Many people shy away from networking because it makes them feel fake or phony—an issue that is particularly difficult for introverts. To combat this feeling, focus on mutual interests and learning about other people, departments, or organizations. These do not even necessarily need to fall within the professional realm; discussion topics could be personal interests that may or may not eventually evolve into professional relationships.

Also, **be curious and ask questions. People love to talk about themselves and what they do.** Even if you are meeting with someone within your technical expertise, there is always an opportunity to learn something new. Focusing on learning, mutual interests, and being curious ensures you are establishing a balanced relationship. You will develop a better understanding for exactly the product or services that others may provide, as well as discovering their ideal client demographic so that you are better able to provide helpful information and relevant referrals.

Always give value first to build and maintain a strong network, rather than attempting to take from new relationships for immediate gain. This becomes easier as you network more. As you meet more new people, you grow in your ability to connect people together and facilitate matching others and your own interests to new opportunities. Making great connections is how you learn and develop from your network, which should be your ultimate goal. Financial benefits come afterward, and they will come if you network well. Most importantly, external networks should be built before you need them.

Do you cultivate and share your network?

Collaboration

Practically every corner of the world is aware of the Golden Rule: "Do unto others as you would have done unto you." Problems with this rule occur when leading people with differing personalities, backgrounds, and talents. The Golden Rule does not necessarily work for everyone all the time. You need to manage, motivate, and treat others the way they want to be treated. This is why the Platinum Rule was coined: "**Do unto others as they would have you do unto them.**"

Collaboration is the process of working together to achieve a common purpose or goal. Effectively working together is generally easier and more productive when those involved follow the Platinum Rule. Your own personality style and your team members' personality styles affect how you likely will interact with each other. Recognizing these tendencies can help leaders predict behavior to adapt, build up, manage, or intervene. As you and your team develop an understanding of personality styles, you will be able to interact with people more effectively and improve collaboration.

When you consider personality styles, it's fascinating how different people value different traits. For example, some find traits such as patience to be more valuable, whereas others find traits such as decisiveness to be more valuable. Your own personality style determines what traits you find more or less valuable in others.

There are four main personality styles: (1) analytical, (2) driver, (3) amiable, and (4) expressive. Each of these personality styles exhibits unique general characteristics, strengths, and weaknesses that need to be managed and engaged in subtly different ways. Understanding these unique characteristics will help you successfully manage differing personality styles on your team to increase collaboration and reach organizational goals.

Analytical

The *Analytical* personality style is very deep and thoughtful. As the name suggests, Analyticals tend to overanalyze everything and be perfectionists. They are serious and purposeful individuals. They set very high standards of performance both personally and professionally. Analyticals are orderly and organized. They also tend to have a dry but witty sense of humor.

Analytical strengths might include that they are perfectionists. They want things done right and they want them done right the first time. They are neat and tidy individuals, economical, and self-disciplined.

Analytical weaknesses show up in the form of being moody, critical, and negative. Analyticals can be indecisive and may overanalyze most things. Their perfectionism can also manifest as a weakness at times because they can be guilty of making their pursuit of perfection stall completion.

To communicate with an Analytical, have your facts straight and be prepared with the correct information. Speak softly and calmly; they do not like loud people in their face. They also appreciate people who give them space, so step back when you are talking to them. As the manager of an Analytical, do not pressure him or her too hard for decisions. When an Analytical says, "I need some time to think about this," the time to think about it is needed. Analyticals are not playing games with you or working a negotiation strategy. They are persuaded by proof, not emotion.

Also practice being in an ask mode when communicating with an analytical person. If your personal personality style is that of a Driver or an Expressive, you may tend to tell rather than to ask. With an Analytical, you want to ask, "What do you think about this? What if we were to do A, B, and C? What are your thoughts?" Analyticals particularly appreciate leaders who think carefully through their decisions and do not take costly shortcuts or make rash decisions for seemingly no reason. A "because I said so" or "because I'm the boss" rationale does not motivate an Analytical team member to be engaged.

If you are a leader or manager with an analytical personality style, you probably want to consider all the facts and variables before you make decisions. But once you have the facts, make a decision. Your followers would rather you made a bad decision than no decision at all, so you need to learn to be more decisive. Also, do not be so negative. If you are an analytical leader or manager, you can often come across as a little bit negative and this will certainly affect your team. Get more involved with people, try to be more social with your team, and be careful of unreasonable standards and your tendency to micromanage. Doing either could be discouraging to your employees or peers. Lighten up about imperfections. They happen!

Driver

Drivers are a dynamic and active personality style. They exude confidence and naturally gravitate toward leadership positions. They move very quickly to action, but they are not detail-oriented. Drivers are great with the big picture—they can be visionaries and are apt to see how they are going to get to where they need to go, but they are not always great at taking the interim steps needed to get there.

You can probably see how an Analytical and a Driver might not always respond well to each other's style but that their skills can nicely complement each other. It can be said that if you want to get to the moon, you hire a Driver; but if you want to get back, you hire an Analytical.

Beth, the vice president of information technology (IT) for a distribution organization based in North America, was experiencing a problem with one of her direct reports. She dreaded meeting with him because he would get into so much detail and never get to the point. John managed the systems architecture group, which was a highly technical job. John excelled in this position because he was so detail-oriented and thorough. He was very capable in designing and estimating technical solutions that required the right size and type of servers and other necessary hardware for various system projects.

Beth recognized these strengths in John, but cringed at the thought of having to meet with him. He would arrive for his weekly status reports and get right into every detail of each project, existing server capacities, what was working, what was not, where potential issues may arise, and so forth. But within the first few minutes of his report, Beth would be checked out, thinking about other key priorities within her department. It got to the point that she would move or cancel meetings and do her best to avoid him.

During one of her leadership training classes, Beth learned about these different personality styles and the key differences for communication and thought patterns. Beth was a Driver, and she realized that this was perhaps the solution to the issues she was experiencing with John back at the office. John was an Analytical, and they were both communicating with each other in their own personality styles rather than adapting to enable more effective collaboration.

Drivers' strengths include determination. They also are typically independent and productive. Drivers get a lot of things done. A Driver would rather make a bad decision than no decision. They have a high sense of urgency and are normally unsettled until a decision is made.

Their weaknesses may include being insensitive, unsympathetic, harsh, proud, or sarcastic. Drivers do not like to admit when they are wrong. They can also rush to a decision without thoroughly thinking through or understanding the results or consequences of their decisions.

To communicate with a Driver, the first thing you need to do is pick up your pace and get to the point. Drivers do not need all the facts and data that Analyticals need. They just want the bottom line or the big picture first. Beth did not want or need all the detailed information that John was presenting to her during their weekly meetings. She just wanted those key insights or issues that gave her the big-picture view of what was going on in John's department. This disconnect was inhibiting her ability to develop a positive relationship with John, who was a very important member of her team.

With her personality styles knowledge, Beth decided to meet with John to coach him on how he could communicate with her more effectively. She began the meeting by recognizing the value that he brought to the organization by always being on top of his responsibilities and projects, never missing any of the important little details that others might have overlooked. Then, she coached him on how to adjust the format of their weekly update meetings so that they would be more mutually productive.

From then on, rather than starting by diving into the minute details of his various projects, John would start his update with the big picture—here are the projects, their status, and one or two important concerns, if any. After his high-level overview, he would allow Beth to ask clarifying questions if she needed more information.

By applying her leadership training, this simple conversation with her manager completely changed the dynamic of Beth and John's relationship. Their better understanding of each other's personality styles allowed them to collaborate on initiatives and greatly improved their relationship. John was later promoted to the director of IT largely due to his demonstrated ability to flex his communication style along with his impressive technical knowledge and abilities.

If you are Driver manager, you are likely the type of leader that is very task-oriented and focused on completing jobs. Be careful of how demanding you can be, and get over your need to debate and correct everybody. Because Drivers may not like to admit when they are wrong, you may find yourself correcting people over things that really do not matter. It is okay that you want to get things done and you want to correct people over things that do matter, but stop arguing over the little things. Also, curb your sarcasm, if that applies to you, and practice listening to people. Drivers tend to formulate responses in their minds while the other person is talking. Be mindful of that, and really work on your active listening skills.

If you are managing a Driver, practice being in task mode, because Drivers want to get things done. Also, let them take the lead and give them more responsibility. Show Drivers appreciation by showing gratitude for their ability to execute—just do not waste too much time trying to pat a Driver on the back, because they don't need it. Drivers appreciate leaders who will let them find the most successful path for reaching their goals, and they despise being micromanaged.

Amiable

The *Amiable* personality style can be a patient and well-balanced individual. They are often quiet but witty. They can be very sympathetic, kind, and inoffensive—Amiables do not like to offend people.

An Amiable is easygoing, and everybody typically likes the Amiables. You know why? It's because they don't like conflict, so they are very easy to get along with. They are diplomatic and calm. But Amiables can also be stubborn and selfish. Their aversion to offence and conflict can also manifest as a weakness when conflict needs to be addressed and managed.

Amiables do not appreciate abrasiveness, so as their manager be considerate rather than brash. When you drop a project in an amiable person's lap at the last minute and say, "I need this today by noon," you're going to cause a tremendous amount of stress. Even show an extra level of kindness. Amiables also need encouragement when taking risks, and this is when you can help them as their manager. Coach them through taking more risk in their jobs, but be aware that Amiables really will try to avoid conflict. They will self-soothe, but they will not want to deal with the conflict that is right in front of them. Amiables appreciate leaders who work closely with them and are kind and considerate.

If you are an Amiable manager, you need to work on sharing your opinions and take a stand on issues. Your team would rather that you disagree with them than not have an opinion about the issues at all. Push yourself to take some risks. You also need to work on being able to address disciplinary issues and conflict in the workplace. Work on your self-motivation; sometimes it is easier for you to procrastinate than it is to jump on a project.

Expressive

The *Expressive* members of the team are the social specialists because they love to have fun. They are individuals who turn disaster into humor, they prevent dull moments, and they can be very generous people. They want to be included on projects, on teams, and in conversations.

When communicating with Expressives, lighten up and have a sense of humor with your expressive team members. Show appreciation for their sense of humor and charisma. Expressives are very outgoing. They can be ambitious, charismatic, and persuasive. But, they can also be disorganized, undisciplined, loud, and incredibly talkative. Expressives can talk up to 200 words per minute with gusts up to 300. They can talk! Expressives need encouragement to check their facts because they tend to exaggerate a little bit.

Although they do need some structure in their jobs, Expressives do not need detailed methods. They appreciate freedom in the workplace, like the Driver. Expressives really want you to allow and show some excitement in the workplace as their manager.

If you are an Expressive manager, you want to be an initiator. Reserve your opinion and do not interrupt people when they are talking. Be careful of exaggerations and exercise more patience with your team. You also need to work on your follow-through. Expressives like to start big, complicated projects and then they get bored with them. This can become very frustrating for your team members, who will be the ones responsible for the details of completing projects.

These are generalizations, and many people will exhibit some amount of any number of these personality styles. However, everyone will more strongly exhibit characteristics of one type over all the others. Recognizing and understanding which personality styles you are managing on your team will help you motivate and communicate with team members.

Managing personality styles can be a challenging part of managing. However, it is likely that you will have a mix of personality styles on your team, and the diversity can expose the strengths of team members and the synergies that come from working together. For example, you do not want a project team of all Drivers or just Drivers and Expressives on a big, complex problem. You need the Analyticals to help make informed decisions, make incremental plans, and keep the project on task. You also need the Amiables to keep the team working together collaboratively. Also, you would be perceptive to include Drivers and Expressives because they help the Analyticals and the Amiables see the big-picture end result, keep the morale and energy high to achieve the goal, and drive the project forward instead of getting stuck in the little details.

As Beth's story demonstrates, you must be aware of the various personality styles of your team members. Understand their style strengths and challenges and be prepared to coach your team on how to effectively communicate with you and each other.

Fostering collaboration within the team requires identifying and understanding how each personality style is motivated and how they communicate, and sharing that understanding with the team. It requires helping others to value the strengths of everyone on the team and to flex both their own and your communication to best build understanding and engagement.

Do you understand and adapt to the various personality styles and working styles within your team?

Conflict Management

Two farmers live next door to each other. Farmer Bob is standing in his kitchen. He looks outside and he sees Farmer John's chicken wander over to his property, lay an egg, and then wander home. So, Farmer Bob goes out to the edge of the property, bends down, and picks up the egg—and when he stands up, he is face to face with Farmer John.

Farmer John says, "Hand it over. That's my egg." To which Farmer Bob responds, "No, it's not. The chicken wandered over to my property and laid the egg, therefore it's my egg." Farmer John replies, "No. It's my chicken, therefore it's my egg."

Farmer Bob says, "Listen, where I come from there's only one way to resolve conflict like this. We take turns punching each other in the stomach as hard as we can five times. The first person to give up loses." Farmer John agrees, "Let's go."

Farmer Bob balls up his fist, the one without the egg in it, swings back, and takes five hard punches to Farmer John's stomach as hard as he can. When he is finished, Farmer John lets out a cough and he says, "Okay, my turn." Farmer Bob holds out his hand and says, "I quit. You can keep your stupid egg."

Disputes don't always end well, but they can. Conflict resolution skills are important for everyone to enjoy a better life, but they are especially important for managers and leaders to be more effective in their jobs. A manager can spend as much as 40 percent of his or her time managing conflict in the workplace.[6] Just imagine what you could achieve if you could use that time doing something else!

Two of the most common misconceptions about conflict are that all conflict is bad and that conflict resolution is about everyone winning. Conflict that is approached constructively and in a healthy way can be good conflict. Good conflict causes us to look at why we might be holding personal views and opinions so tightly. It also helps us find a way to live and work more peacefully with other people.

Give up the concept of winning in conflict management. Resolving conflict does not mean that everyone is going to win. It is about process and ensuring that everyone feels his or her voice and opinion have been heard and considered. The best conflict managers approach conflict with open perspectives, and they ask more questions than others. They believe in the value of preserving relationships and understand that compromising is not a sign of weakness but in many instances is a sign of strength and perspective. Living and working peacefully and productively with others does not necessarily mean that all will agree with one another or that conflicts will not arise.

Conflict resolution is another common myth about conflict. You might have a fundamental values difference with somebody that cannot be resolved, and all the arguing in the world is not going to change either party's mind. The only way forward in this scenario (which does happen often) is to stop arguing and realize that the issue or topic is going to remain unresolved. This does not mean that you cannot continue to show kindness and respect toward someone with whom you fundamentally disagree. As the saying goes, **"You can disagree without being disagreeable."** Being respectful is always your primary aim.

Values-based conflict can be difficult to resolve, and personality conflict is often considered impossible to overcome. In reality, personality conflict often can be resolved. You may think that you will never get along with someone with whom you have a personality conflict. Personality style conflict does take a high level of emotional intelligence to resolve, but it is possible to achieve when you develop your ability to understand your own personality style and the personality styles of associates. The better you adapt, the more likely you can build a productive team with productive relationships.

Developing conflict management skills takes time, but is made easier by using the dialogue method. This tool was originated by Harville Hendrix, PhD, and author of relationship books. To improve professional and personal relationships and handle conflict more effectively, use the six steps of the dialogue method, illustrated with the following scenario.

It is a Thursday morning and your direct report walks into your office very upset with you because you promoted someone else and he feels like he deserved it. Angry, he vents his frustrations over all the long hours and extra projects he has taken on for the organization, not to mention the late nights and missed sporting events of his children. He has given almost every waking moment for what? Nothing! This is when you start step 1 of the dialogue method.

You quietly **listen and let him vent** his frustrations. This is the most challenging step for you because your first response may be to get defensive. Instead, you invite him to sit down and talk. He continues to vent his anger until finally taking a breath and a break.

This is when you move to step 2 of the dialogue method. You **mirror back, or repeat**, what he was saying. "So, what I hear you saying is that you're very frustrated. You feel like you should have been promoted. You don't understand why he got promoted, and you feel like you've been here longer with more experience. Am I hearing you correctly?" By mirroring back, you are containing his anger and showing that you were listening to his concerns and frustrations.

Then, you go to step 3, you **ask for more**. This is a tough one, but you ask him: "What else? What else is frustrating you about this situation?" He might expand on his earlier statements, saying something like, "Well, I'm also frustrated that I don't feel like anybody around here really appreciates me." And then you mirror those statements back as well. Then, move to step 4.

Step 4 is to **validate**. You validate his feelings by saying, "It makes sense that you would feel that way." Validating his feelings shows him that you respect the way that he is feeling, that his feelings are neither right nor wrong. Once you have validated, you move right into step 5, which is to **empathize**. Empathizing takes it one step further; you try to determine what the person also might be feeling. You say, "I would imagine you might also be feeling like, 'Why do I even try around here. Does it even matter to anybody?' Are you feeling that way?" He says, "Yes, I am feeling that way." Now you move to the last step of the dialogue method.

Step 6 is **response**. You start by saying, "Would it be okay if I respond?" At this point, you have gone through all the steps and given him a chance to be heard. You will have set up a constructive environment for making a reasonable response. While following the six steps of the dialogue method, be aware that there also are six barriers to conflict resolution that are, in our human nature, common reactions in conflict situations.

The Six Barriers to Conflict Resolution

1. Getting defensive
2. Dismissing the topic as unimportant
3. Jumping to conclusions
4. Not listening
5. Not empathizing
6. Not staying calm

Think about these six barriers. Managers should attempt to resolve conflicts before they become too large and before the individuals involved are wasting too much negative energy over friction, which may be settled through constructive communication and understanding.

When in conflict situations, how many of the six barriers do you sometimes violate?

It is a natural reaction to want to avoid conflict or to get defensive in the face of conflict. The problem is that when you avoid conflict or become defensive you are effectively adding fuel to the fire. Your defensive response will only fan the flames, while also limiting your ability to really listen to and understand the other person's perspective on the issue. In other words, it closes the door. Keep the door of two-way communication open. Instead of becoming defensive, force yourself to remain quiet and listen to what the other party has to say—really listen to them. If necessary, encourage them to provide you with more feedback on their view.

Dismissing the topic as unimportant sounds something like this: "You're making too big of a deal out of this" or "You shouldn't feel that way." If somebody comes to you with a conflict and the person is venting his or her frustrations and you respond in this way, you are dismissing the topic as unimportant. **If it's important to them, it needs to become important to you.** Feelings are neither right nor wrong, they are simply information. Never say something like, "You shouldn't feel that way." Instead of dismissing their feelings, get to the root of why they are feeling that way. Do this by asking for more information and then repeating back to them what you have just heard. Make sure you understand their perspective on the issue clearly and that they receive validation they are being listened to. Remember, it is not about whether their perspective and feelings are right or wrong, it is simply about understanding where the conflict is coming from.

Refraining from jumping to conclusions is challenging. Jumping to conclusions can stem from our own defensiveness, particularly if the conflict is about us personally. Faulty conclusions can also arise when you are mediating conflict, for example when two employees are in conflict. Make sure you get the other side of the story and reserve judgment until you have heard all sides of the story. Sometimes, it is prudent to invite a third party to give insight by telling an outsider's version of the story, especially when there are others who might add helpful perspectives.

It is very common to mentally prepare for a comeback instead of listening. The problem, like many of these other barriers, is that managers may not allow one or another person to be heard, and reacting in that way erases the opportunity to hear and understand relevant perspectives. Active listening in any conflict situation allows each party involved in the conflict space to de-escalate the tone of the conflict, become less aggressive, and signal to the other person that he or she is respected. Instead of trying to think of what you are going to say in response, make yourself stop and listen. Repeat back what you understood, both to signal to the other person that you are indeed listening and to make sure you do in fact understand what he or she saying.

Empathizing may be difficult, particularly in a conflict situation in which one person is clearly wrong. However, having empathy has little to do with whether that person is right or wrong. Empathizing signals to others that they have been heard and understood. Empathizing does not have to be a drawn-out monologue; it is more about identifying that you are aware of how the other person is feeling.

There are times when situations explode and conflict escalates. You might detect that as people raise their voices, become more aggressive, and possibly shift into attack mode. You might even begin to lose your control in this scenario. But, you must maintain control and make sure never to lose your temper in heated situations. This is perhaps the most damaging barrier. Good conflict managers stop and think before speaking or doing. Ask yourself, "Will this help or hinder the situation?" Generally, a lowered voice and calmness will help calm excitable situations. **Create a safe place where people can openly express their opinions, and be sure your responses only include the facts, without exaggeration or bias.** These steps will keep you from adding fuel to the fire, and hopefully enable you to de-escalate issues so that everyone can move forward with a resolution.

Not every conflict will have a resolution in which everyone wins. However, there are good tools available for effectively managing conflict and resolving these issues in such a way that all individuals involved can walk away feeling their voices have been heard and that they have been treated respectfully.

Networking, collaboration, and conflict management contribute directly to developing positive relationships, and these three skills are normally not accomplished as easily as sipping tea. But often, leaders who have developed positive relationship-building skills have been seeped in experiences. Learn from your own experiences and from observing the experiences of others.

Core Competency: Develops Positive Relationships

Builds partnerships and effective working relationships to meet shared objectives. Recognizes and shows respect for people, ideas, and perspectives that differ from self. Actively seeks to positively resolve interpersonal disagreement and conflict.

Competency Skills
- **Collaboration:** Builds partnerships and works collaboratively with others to achieve shared objectives
- **Networking:** Establishes relationship networks and alliances inside and outside of organization
- **Conflict Management:** Encourages differences of opinions. Anticipates, manages, and resolves conflict in a constructive manner

---

Develops Positive Relationships Assessment Questions

1. Are you known as someone who helps others in the organization?
2. Do you cultivate and share your network?
3. Do you understand and adapt to the various personality styles and working styles within your team?
4. When in conflict situations, how many of the six barriers do you sometimes violate?

The Leader's Toolkit

1. A fun team-building exercise: Understanding Personality Styles Within a Team.
   a. Review the characteristics of the four personality styles (Analytical, Driver, Amiable, Expressive) with the group.
   b. Create a summary slide or handout with the style descriptors.

    c. Clarify that all styles are needed for an effective team. No one style is better than another style.

    d. Each team member selects the style that best describes him or her but does not disclose the style to other team members.

    e. Have team members tape a blank piece of paper on their backs. Each team member guesses the style of the other person and writes the style name, along with a few words about why the style was selected, on their team member's paper. For example, Analytical: likes to get into the details.

    f. Once everyone has completed the rounds, allow team members to remove the sheet from their back and review, but without comments.

    g. Have the group stand in a circle and proceed with the first person: "Sally. What do you think Sally's style is?" The group calls out what style they believe the person is and then the person reveals his or her style.

    h. Proceed until everyone's style has been revealed.

2. Build an external networking schedule and commit to have coffee with one new person per week. Ask your new contacts who in their network they would recommend you to meet. Offer to connect them to your network as well. Diagram your network in terms of types of industry, experience, and what help the individuals are seeking. Also, be sure to record the date you met them, as well as a follow-up date.

8

Develops Customer Focus

S hampoo was invented in India. Turn back time to the 1500s and boil a few soapberries with dried gooseberries to make the concoction that would clean your hair. The product name itself is derived from the Sanskrit word *champu*.

Today, you can buy the modern *champu* in hundreds of brands and you get to pick the formula: dandruff, moisturizing, straightening, oily hair, chelating, clarifying, detoxifying, smoothing, soothing, all-natural, gluten-free, wheat-free, sulfate-free, antibacterial, color protection, gentle baby, jelly, paste, cream, or powder.

No shampoo makes claims like, "not likely to clean your hair" or "will probably give you disappointing results." The claims are always about the positive customer experience.

The pattern is similar with business claims. Organizations of all kinds rarely claim anything but the best presentation of themselves. The way this often appears in business is in the claim that an organization or company is *focused on the customer or always delivering customer service excellence*.

It's natural to view your own customer service as above average, but compared to what? It's clear that customer service means different things to different people.

Shampoos that clean hair and businesses that claim to provide excellent customer service both follow formulas, and the styles of customer service come in as many varieties as shampoos. At a basic level, shampoo promises to clean your hair, and we would all be dissatisfied if it did not. At another basic level, organizations are expected to deliver whatever they promise, and we generally are surprised when that does not happen.

But basic level is not enough in business. Leaders and the teams they manage in competitive marketplaces must do more than meet expectations. Tangible ingredients like water and detergents appear in most hair-cleaning products, but creating a customer experience that propels your business forward is all about the intangible ingredients, and there are three essential ingredients that excellent leaders consistently manage well: (1) trust and credibility, (2) needs and opportunity awareness, and (3) responsive problem solving.

Developing customer focus starts with the desire to master all three of these, and desire is linked to attitude. When managers embrace the possibility that the customer experience can be improved, they are likely to do more than meet expectations.

Trust and Credibility

Fill in the blank on this statement: My customers expect _____.
Fill in the blank with the things in your line of work that your customers expect from your organization to be satisfied.

Your brand develops trust and credibility with your customers when their expectations are, at least, being met. What do people expect? They expect timeliness; they expect accuracy; they expect to be heard; and they expect to leave happy. But where do customer expectations come from? Customer expectations come from previous experiences—both experiences with your organization and experiences with your competitors. If they have replaced one of your competitors with you, or are contemplating doing so, they will absolutely be comparing their experiences with you with those of your competitors. The bar has already been set at some level for many of your customers, and if the bar is not being met they are not going to be satisfied.

Your customers also experience great customer service from other organizations that are not your competitors. They may have nothing to do with your product, service, or industry at all. Because the world has evolved into a customer-centric environment, customers have a certain level of customer service expectation overall. Their previous experiences affect their expectations of every organization from which they receive services, including your organization. **Do not overlook how other organizations outside or within your industry are developing and managing customer focus to gain insights on customer satisfaction gaps that could result in a competitive advantage.**

Customers also develop expectations from your own marketing and sales department. Your market communications—brand promise, advertising, content, and direct communications—all work together to bring customers in and establish an initial impression and a presumption of the service that you should provide for them in the future. These communications must align with the reality of your organization's ability to deliver on these expectations and your brand promise. If your marketing and sales departments are making promises that your organization is not able to fulfill, you may be dissolving your brand's trust and credibility in the market. In fact, **once a customer is lost, it is very hard to win him or her back**.

> What is your customer's satisfaction score? Do you know the one key change that would improve this score?

Needs and Opportunity Awareness

A public service ferry operator in Canada was losing money every year, so new management was brought in, analyzed the situation, and decided that the only realistic way to stop losing money was to increase revenue. They decided to begin by surveying current customers to find out what it would take to have them use the ferry more often. The feedback they received was very negative. They heard that the ferry was beaten up and rundown, they were unpleasant, and the piers smelled bad. People only took the ferry because they had to. If there was any other way to get where they needed to go, they would not take the ferry. The food on the ferry was lousy, and they felt that the crew treated them like cattle.

The survey allowed them to assess the needs of their customers and determine that the greatest areas of opportunity clearly were to improve the facilities and the service. They succeeded in persuading the county commissioners that there needed to be a budget developed to improve the situation before they could increase revenue, so they budgeted money and refurbished the boats and the piers. They also recognized the need to invest in developing the employees' customer service skills.

Most of the time, a customer complains for a very good reason. The organization made service promises that were not kept, and the customer is right to complain. In fact, very few customers complain directly to your organization, so when someone steps up and gives you the chance to make things right, it opens up a real opportunity to win back his or her trust. These customers are helping you become aware of their needs, which are not being met, and are providing you with an opportunity to correct and improve their experience with you.

Instead of bringing someone in or signing employees up for a 1-day training workshop, the ferry operator framed it as an opportunity for professional development that the employees had never been provided with before. This instilled a sense of engagement and pride in the employees. Employees felt valued and a part of a winning team—a team the organization was willing to invest in.

The ferry organization named their development program "The Mastery of Customer Service Certificate" program. It was a long-term, ongoing program and after each module the participants would get a badge or a diploma. The program was strongly supported and encouraged by top management, so these were perceived as high points of pride and further motivated and engaged employees in improving. As a result of improving the facilities, refurbishing the ferries, and developing their employees, they had huge increases in customer satisfaction and improved their financial position significantly. Revenues went up 33 percent across the board, which meant people were using it repeatedly. It also indicated that they were telling their friends about the ferry, and their friends were coming more often to the pier and using the ferry as an attraction. Concession sales also improved to account for a 20 percent revenue increase in addition to the 33 percent increase they experienced from increased ridership.

Needs assessment and opportunity awareness help to make big improvements for an organization. As with the ferry operator, **many of the problems that customers have with products and services actually are predictable**. Although it is a good idea to survey your customers to get specific feedback (and to engage customers in improving your brand), there are likely areas of your organization that you can already identify as common Coffee Stains or problems for customers. The managers of the ferry likely took one look at the facilities and had a sense that the rundown ferries and piers were a contributing factor to customer dissatisfaction before receiving any feedback directly from customers. As a leader, assessing and understanding which problems are predictable and then preparing a proactive recovery action plan is a great opportunity.

How are you proactively anticipating and resolving customer problems?

Think about the most common complaints you hear within your organization. These are easily identifiable patterns and may indicate where your organization is not keeping promises that were made to your customers. Think about how you can put a plan in place for dealing with these predictable problems that surface over and over.

The airline industry is a great example of how leaders can create an opportunity out of a predictable problem. On very popular routes, airlines have more demand than they have seats; unfortunately, customers who have paid for the seats sometimes do not show up. The reason often is because their plans changed at the last minute or because the airline's incoming flight was not on time. When this happens, very popular flights have flown with empty seats that cost revenue for the airline. In response to that situation, airlines deliberately overbook some flights. For the most part, overbooking flights works because people do not show up or cancel. But airlines also sometimes have unhappy customers who arrive at a gate only to find out that they have no guaranteed seat, even though every one of those customers paid for a ticket.

So how do the airlines handle this predictable problem? They each may handle it differently, but generally they pay people not to get on the overbooked flight. Gate agents can often be heard enticing willing passengers to take a later flight in exchange for something. The minute they anticipate a seating problem, they start making announcements like, "We have good news. We are in an oversold situation. A lucky person is going to get a free round trip ticket to any place he or she likes and an upgrade on the next flight out. If you would like to volunteer, please step up." This approach is a whole lot better than waiting until the very end, hoping that someone will not show up at the gate.

Of course, there is some cost associated with this solution for airlines, but the **cost balances out when customer satisfaction, loyalty, and value are factored in**. With your predictable problems, the resolution may have some cost associated with it, but if you truly believe in the value of a loyal customer, the lifetime value of repeated purchases, and the value of a good reputation, you can see the value in developing solutions for predictable customer problems.

Because you will not be there for every single customer problem that comes up, the logical next requirement is to teach your employees how to solve customer problems effectively and with competence and empathy. Predictable problems present an opportunity to create a plan, and then your employees need to be trained to use that plan. It is true that you cannot train people for every situation— not all problems are predictable. For unpredictable problems, you need to train your employees on effective problem solving, and then empower them to do whatever it takes to solve the problem.

Responsive Problem Solving

Stellar service organizations empower their employees to do whatever it takes to solve the problem. One example is a department store chain that tells its employees to **use your own best judgment at all times**. Another company, a luxury hotel chain, has a budget to solve customer problems. They know that losing a customer averages $100,000 in lost revenue over the life of the customer. Rather than risking that, they empower employees with a preapproved budget to solve the problem without needing to aggravate the customer further by waiting for approvals for solutions. They can just fix the problem.

What is the lifetime value of one of your key customers?

On average, if a customer's complaint is effectively addressed, the customer will tell six or more people about their positive experience. But if their complaint is not handled properly, they will tell 15 more people about it. In the meantime, only one out of every 26 unhappy customers will complain to the organization; most will simply leave or never return.[7]

For many organizations, dissatisfaction can lead to negative viral postings potentially read by a much wider audience; however, most of the real danger of customer dissatisfaction is hidden from view, so do not become complacent. Do not be afraid of customer problems but rather seek them out through surveys, reviews, and direct outreach. Poor customer reviews are an opportunity to improve, and the capacity to solve problems is what makes a manager a successful transformational leader.

The main principle in solving customer problems is to treat the person, then the problem. And the sequence of that is extremely important. By treating the person first, you can defuse anger and give him or her a chance to settle down so that you can solve the problem effectively. Skipping that step in your eagerness to immediately solve the problem might make the situation worse; by the time a customer has gotten angry enough to complain to you, the customer is probably emotional about the situation as well.

When customers have a negative experience, they are usually going to react. Because that reaction may cause them to get upset, you may start to see changes in the way that they look and behave. The very excited ones will start vocalizing their frustrations. Sometimes, they will talk on and on about the issue, repeating themselves, and it can be tempting at this point to interject. But if you try to interrupt them, argue, or get defensive—or if you try to tell them things they are not be ready to hear—there is a good chance that you will only be making matters worse. Because the very angry customers need to first vent their frustrations, it does not particularly matter what apology or solution you promptly give. The best thing you can do is sincerely and genuinely listen without interrupting.

Once they have vented, they may pause and look at you as if to say, "So what are you going to do about it?" The first words out of your mouth ought to be: "**I apologize for the service breakdown.**" There has been a lot of thought given to that phrase, and there is a reason why it is so effective. When customers complain to you or to a member of your team, do the customers think they deserve an apology? Absolutely, so when the first words out of your mouth or spoken by your associate are "I apologize," you have given customers the first thing they wanted to receive. By adding "for the service breakdown" You acknowledge that the customer has a legitimate complaint of some kind, even though the situation has not yet been addressed.

To say "I apologize for the service breakdown," conveys that what they have experienced is not normally how your organization conducts business. It conveys that this is an unusual failure in your process, which gives the customer some assurance. Also, saying "I apologize for the service breakdown," does not place blame on anyone, any department, or any other people. Modify the phrase for your team if needed. If you want to say "I'm sorry" instead of "I apologize," do so, but use the phrase "for the service breakdown" to set the stage for better problem resolution.

The next important element of the process of treating the person is to reflect back the concerns expressed so that you acknowledge the content as well as the customer's feelings. The opportunity for managers is to create a full team of employees who both know how to respond in this way and will do so when customers complain. Parroting what the customer says word for word is not the goal; in fact, that would be condescending and counterproductive. In some disagreeable customer situations, it might be appropriate to say, "You know, you're right about that." And that, instead of the arguments and defensiveness they may have been expecting, may induce them to feel that you are on their side.

At this point, you have listened without interrupting; you apologized for the service breakdown; and you reflected back that you understood the customer was upset. You have acknowledged the customer's feelings. These are the steps that good leaders use to reduce or end combativeness.

> When dealing with customer conflicts, do you treat the person first and then the problem?

Most likely, anyone who has worked in construction services knows that customer service issues can get a little heated. When subcontractors do not show up or when estimated costs do not match with reality, projects tend to go sideways and emotions flare.

Tony was the superintendent on a construction site in the United States and conveyed a message to the offsite project manager who was the overseer representing the customer. When the project manager called later, Tony relied on customer service training he had received from his leadership development program.

"I got your update this morning, Tony, and you can't be expecting me to just let this fly!" The project manager began his tirade and continued.

Applying his angry-customer response training, Tony remained quiet and allowed the project manager to vent. For almost 10 minutes he waited patiently, listening, as the project manager hurled anger, accusations, and insulting language at Tony and his employer. When the project manager finally settled down, Tony responded:

"I apologize for the service breakdown."

Working through this method, Tony and the project manager could move forward with fixing the issue that had led to this confrontation. By the end of it, the project manager said to Tony, "You know what? An hour ago, I was so mad I could have cut you guys off right then and there. But now . . . I'm impressed. You handled that extremely well. I like working with companies like yours. I have two more jobs and I'd like you guys to do that work." This solution led to $600,000 in new business without Tony's company submitting a bid!

There is always the possibility though that an employee or you might not actually know how to solve the customer's problem. It might not be obvious, so a good solution is to ask the customer. You might say, "I want to do whatever it takes to make this right. What do you think is a fair solution?" Ask them and then do whatever it takes to satisfy the customer.

Doing whatever it takes to satisfy the customer has been a somewhat controversial topic. Many managers are concerned about customers trying to take advantage of these situations. And it is true, sometimes customers will try to take advantage. They might complain when there is not really a problem, sometimes to defraud. Although some customer complaints are disingenuous, **customer complaints are valid 98 percent of the time.** So, to allow the 2 percent to dictate how you handle all or most of your customer complaints is a poor approach if your desire is to be an excellent service organization and create a customer base of delighted, loyal brand advocates. Consider it a cost of doing business, a cost of service recovery that occasionally there will be a customer who takes advantage of you.

Although conventional wisdom suggests that the customer is never wrong, there are instances when customers are simply mistaken of the facts. This presents an interesting challenge to some, but there is a good solution that can be illustrated by an exchange between an employee and a customer.

A clerk at a home improvement store was asked to help a customer pick out a small heater. The helpful clerk asked, "How large is the room?" and the customer said it is roughly 8 feet square or 2.4 meters square. So, the clerk walked with the customer to the merchandise and picked up a boxed heater and said, "This will be just perfect for your room." The customer looked at the box skeptically and said, "There is no way that tiny little space heater will be able to heat up my room."

The clerk knew that it was the right size. He knew the customer was wrong, but he did not argue with the customer. Instead he replied, "You know, you might be right about that. Let's have a look." So, he handed the box to the customer, and the customer read the label where the heat output and room size were summarized.

"Wow. This really must be a powerful little unit," the customer said as he read the packaging. The clerk replied, "I have had nothing but satisfied customers."

That approach is much different from telling customers that they are wrong, and it is called diplomatic disagreement. You are not disagreeing with them directly and you are not telling them they are wrong or that you know better than they do. You are being very effective in getting them to come to the correct conclusion, to decide for themselves that the solution makes sense.

There are times when customers may be dissatisfied about things that are out of a manager's control. A common example of this type of situation concerns price. A customer was in a hardware store complaining about the price of a crescent wrench to an employee. "This is too high, no one pays that much for one lousy crescent wrench!" The employee responded thoughtfully, "I'm sorry, sir. Where did you get the idea that this is too much for a crescent wrench of that brand?" The question made the customer pause for a moment. Perplexed, he asked, "What do you mean?"

This gave the employee the chance to explain some of the specific features of the crescent wrench in question. He said, "This one comes with a lifetime warranty; it's rustproof; and they claim it's breakproof, so if it ever breaks or rusts you can bring it back for a refund." He added, "We have a lot of other less-expensive crescent wrenches, but that's the story behind this one." He took the complaint as an opportunity to educate the customer. Attempting to pressure customers into buying something they do not want is far less profitable than engaging them in reasonable conversations. Train your team to use these opportunities to build relationships with the customers.

Another beneficial approach to resolving customer service issues is the widely known *feel, felt, found* technique. When a customer expresses concerns or objections, well-trained team members can show empathy, affirm any concerns or objections, and then ease the customer into moving beyond concerns. The first step is to acknowledge that you understand how the customer currently feels, then acknowledge that others like them have felt that same way in the past. Those two steps establish the *feel* and *felt* parts of the technique. The first shows empathy. The second authenticates the customer's perception or concern by relating the customer's feelings to the past perceptions or concerns of others. The third step can help customers see themselves moving forward with your products or services because of the implication that others have *found* your products or services to be beneficial, valuable, or better than expected. For example, a well-trained member of your team can point out that other customers have found value in the product or service. They might say, "When others did their own research (or experienced the product or service) they found that it was a valuable transformation from the process they were using before," or something similar.

Focusing on your customer produces a direct impact on your organization's bottom line. Organizations are far more profitable when they have a loyal customer base. Customers who will repeatedly choose you over competitors are also those who advocate for you to other potential customers in their networks. It's worth the effort to please customers because they have the potential of bringing you more loyal customers at a much lower cost of acquisition. Delivering on your brand promise develops trust and credibility. Customer problems happen for every brand, but the ability to consistently assess needs, resolve problems, capitalize on opportunities, and develop trust makes your brand credible.

Distinguishing your company or organization based on the customer service that you provide requires customer-focused decisions or actions. Those decisions or actions depend on three intangible and essential ingredients that you can enhance, especially through practical training: (1) trust and credibility, (2) responsive problem solving, and (3) awareness of customer needs and opportunities. Managers who excel in this key competency are doing more than boiling a few soapberries with dried gooseberries. Customers expect more, and smart leaders will develop teams that are empowered to astound their clientele.

Core Competency: Develops Customer Focus

Develops and sustains productive customer relationships. Gains insight into customer needs and opportunities, and delivers solutions to exceed customer expectations.

Competency Skills
- **Trust and Credibility:** Builds strong internal and external customer relationships by following through on commitments
- **Responsive Problem Solving:** Anticipates and delivers effective and timely solutions to customer problems
- **Needs and Opportunity Awareness:** Proactively identifies opportunities that benefit internal and external customers

---

Develops Customer Focus Assessment Questions

1. What is your customer's satisfaction score? Do you know the one key change that would improve the score?
2. How are you proactively anticipating and resolving customer problems?
3. What is the lifetime value of one of your key customers?
4. When dealing with customer conflicts, do you treat the person first and then the problem?

The Leader's Toolkit

1. Secret shop your competition and yourself. Review the results with your team and create actions to improve your customer experience. Follow up a few months later by secret shopping yourself again and audit the results—has the customer experience improved?

2. Think about the best customer experience you have had in the past few months. What made the experience exceptional?

   a. Make a list of the elements that you can identify.

   b. Prioritize these elements based on the impact of the elements on your experience.

   c. Compare these elements with your current customer service program and see how you would rate.

   d. Share this exercise with your team.

9

Fosters Innovation

W hat's new and what's next in the competitive coffee industry? Consumers have been inspired by new blends, new concoctions, new packaging, new coffee-brewing conveniences for the home or office, new kinds of advertising, and a thriving new coffee culture.

The growing number of coffee machine designs in production, even mind-reading coffee makers, has flourished because of demand. Companies have used innovative advertising and branding to inspire growing global demand. Coffee companies add value to their own companies by adding value to the customers they serve.

In terms of raising the potential of managers in any organization, innovation itself acts like coffee as a stimulant. Leaders must contribute to and build environments to generate and carry through new ideas that will transform challenges into valuable new ways, new customers, new employee excitement, new solutions, or new revenue.

A coffee bean is actually a seed, and whether the coffee bean is roasted and ground for brewing or planted is a conscious choice. Leaders must make similar decisions about whether to focus on output, for example, or on retooling the way that output is achieved to improve the process and future results. New discoveries that positively affect quality, output, cost, or time first require leaders to be open to different perspectives.

In folklore, people allegedly have believed that the bubbles on the surface of a cup of coffee can predict whether they will prosper or struggle. If the bubbles float toward you, expect good times. But innovation-inclined leaders need levelheaded *change leadership and management, continuous improvement,* and teams and individuals who rely on *complex thinking,* not on superstition.

Former British Prime Minister Harold Wilson once said, "He who rejects change is the architect of decay. The only human institution that justifiably rejects progress is the cemetery." We are creating change more rapidly as a society, and people are open to change now more than ever. The reason that people generally do not resist the change that comes about in technology is, for the most part, the belief that technology improves their lives. People see the change as beneficial and that's one of the key elements that energizes people to embrace it. By identifying and supporting opportunities for change and innovation, leaders improve their organization's chances of remaining relevant in the future.

Change Leadership and Management

Not all change is good. Change leadership involves selecting the key changes that are worth making and then changing the habits and processes that support those changes and allow teams to be effective. Managing the tensions between making changes and honoring tradition is part of the process. Leaders walk the line between helping those who embrace change versus those who do not. Most people do not resist change simply because it is change; people often welcome some changes, such as improved technology, that they believe will have a positive impact on their lives. They resist change when they believe it carries a shortcoming. There are four key reasons people resist change: (1) They do not believe it will benefit them; (2) they do not think the sacrifices they will make will be worth the benefits; (3) they did not help to create the change and lack ownership; and (4) they mistrust the architects behind the change. You can imagine how multiple reasons can apply to one change, compounding dissatisfaction and resistance.

In part, the leadership necessary to create innovation hinges on the way managers have handled changes in the past. A team environment conducive to change evolves as team members feel included, feel supported, and feel safe to engage. Leaders are tested on how well they enact change.

Four Key Reasons People Resist Change

1. They do not believe it will benefit them.
2. They do not think the sacrifices they will make will be worth the benefits.
3. They did not help to create the change and lack ownership.
4. They mistrust the architects behind the change.

Imagine that an organization announced implementation of a new client data management system and told all its employees that the new system promised many benefits, including decreasing the time necessary to complete some of the more labor-intensive tasks.

However, in exchange, employees would also have to come in every weekend for the next year to train on the new system. Transferring all the data over to the new system would also take up to 9 months. Evidently, employees were unaware that the organization was looking for a new system, or even that one was needed. Many employees felt moody over the fact that no one in a management role had bothered to ask the operators if there were any other systems that they might recommend for consideration before the decision had been made and new software purchased. Furthermore, employees were unclear about what would make this new system so much better and more efficient than the one they had been using? The perception among employees was fast becoming negative as individuals wondered, "Is this change beneficial to me? Do the benefits outweigh the sacrifices that I have to make to implement the change (a whole year of weekends!)? Why wasn't I part of the change process, and do I really trust that the leadership did adequate research, or was it an impulsive decision?"

The underlying problem here really is a lack of communication. Without clearly communicating the benefits of the change, there is little hope the organization would succeed in getting immediate acceptance or broad support. Suppose the new system was the best available, and based on analysis, worth the sacrifices required for full implementation. Unfortunately for the change leaders, no one performing the operations understood the need or benefits prior to the change taking place. **George Bernard Shaw famously said, "The single biggest problem in communication is the illusion that is has taken place."** Leaders must communicate clearly the need for change and how employees' jobs will be affected. Influential change leaders always predetermine the benefits that the change will provide to the affected employees. "What is in it for me?" is one of the pertinent questions on the minds of those asked to embrace change.

Not all people go through the change process simultaneously. The start time and the rate of adapting to the new changes directly depend on how close they are to the change. Resistance to change is normal, and the leader's role is to help coach employees through the process.

> Are you communicating and painting a clear picture of the change and the benefits of the change?

If you want to foster innovation, be an effective change leader. Start with trust, because overcoming the resistance and inviting others to imagine and champion new ideas will not get very far if your team does not trust you. It goes without saying that to build better trust you need to be a trustworthy person. This entails being honest, transparent, dependable, confidential, loyal, accountable, and humble. There is a proverb that says, "Trust is like fine china. Once broken, it can be repaired but it is never quite the same." Do not break trust with people by lying to them.

Be proactive in sharing information about changes and more often about where the organization is heading in the future. Innovation is a future-based solution to current challenges or opportunities. Transparency and direct honesty are two leadership strengths that feed innovative cultures. Bring your group together at set times and commit to share information that may be of interest to or affect the members of your team. Dependability also creates trust. Be dependable by doing what you say you are going to do when you said you would do it.

How well does your team trust you? How do you know?

Loyalty and trust form the bedrock for teams to think creatively, and everyone on the team shares responsibility to reimagine how things might be done better or differently to achieve results. Leaders, through their responses and actions, influence how willing team members will be to experiment. Loyal employees who have confidence that their leaders will support innovations will be more likely to unlock hidden ideas that might help the organization improve. Whether team members grow in their loyalties to an organization, to their managers, or to a vision often mirrors their leaders own loyalty to organizational values as well as to their own personal values.

Fostering innovation and change may start with ideas and team characteristics, but ultimately leaders must turn ideas into well-measured action plans. Account-ability becomes the cornerstone for implementing change. Hold yourself account-able for the decisions you make and the decisions your direct reports make on your behalf or with your insistence. **Make yourself accountable up, down, and sideways in your organization. Everyone at every level needs to know you are reliable, and that new ideas will be carried through from inception to full implementation.**

Reliable and trusted leaders maintain the confidence of others by acting humbly and honestly when errors occur. When you know you are wrong, admit it. When you need to apologize, do it. People trust people that they respect and can relate to, and humility is a trait of trustworthy character.

Leaders can enable teams to help through change, starting with its creation. Reduced resistance is the overarching benefit of including team members or associates in the process of developing new and better tools or techniques. When others become part of a decision-making process, they typically have a much stronger personal desire to see it succeed. You may also discover that you can implement far more efficient, beneficial solutions in your organization by involving the people who are working on those tasks and activities every day. When people work together to make change recommendations and innovations, they are more likely to support the process, including any anticipated sacrifices.

One weekend, a manager thought she would do something nice for her employees. They had been frustrated with their work area. They did not like the paint, the plants, the desks. It was all worn out and dilapidated, and they wanted something newer. To give them something special, she hired a team to completely remodel the work area while they were out for the weekend. The manager was excited to see their reactions on Monday morning. When they arrived to work, her excitement turned to disappointment and confusion when they were underwhelmed by the changed workspace.

What the manager soon realized was that, although new, the office makeover was not what members of the team had envisioned. She had never even thought to include them in the design changes because she wanted it to be a surprise.

Some people fear change because they are afraid they might make a mistake, and as a result get into trouble. Humans are creatures of habit, and our brains are hardwired to avoid making mistakes. But making mistakes is an inherent part of transition and change.

According to an engineering principle, when there is movement, there is always some degree of error. When you are driving on a straight road at a high speed, your hand is slightly adjusting back and forth to stay between the lines on the road. Course corrections are a necessary part of moving forward. The leader's responsibility is to see an error as an opportunity for a course correction. Change leaders must create an environment that mitigates the fear of change and is flexible to accommodate new ideas, especially from employees. You can mitigate this fear and foster innovation by clearly setting expectations with your team. Make it safe.

You must expect that mistakes are going to happen when change is happening and when things are in transition. Leave room for mistakes when your team is working through change, and prove to your team that most mistakes are recoverable. Reacting strongly when an employee makes a mistake may steer members of a team to be less willing or less able to cope with important changes in the business, let alone offer new suggestions concerning what might be improved.

The way that leaders respond to errors directly feeds employee trust, loyalty, and the willingness of team members or others to commit. The following example illustrates an exceptional choice by a department director to downplay an error and at the same time build trust, loyalty, confidence, and commitment.

A young man who had just started with the company on the information technology (IT) team was working on the network during his second week on the job when, unexpectedly, the system stopped and every screen in the office went blank. He heard things coming out of other cubicles that were not constructive—and he knew at that moment that he had made a big mistake.

He went directly to his boss and said, "I think I've made a big mistake." She, being an approachable manager, began to ask questions to collect information, "Tell me what happened."

At that moment, from down the hall, came her boss—a loud, angry type of boss—shouting his way through the cubicles. He stormed into the office, red-faced and yelling. The guy who made the mistake was sitting there watching his boss get yelled at for his mistake. In his head, the new IT employee said to himself, "I've only been on the job for two weeks. I'm history. I'm fired for sure."

For 15 minutes, he watched as his boss got yelled at, and not once did she even mention his name. She took the entire heat of that confrontation. Finally, her angry boss began to run out of steam and said, "This mistake should have never happened!" To which she replied, "It did, and I take full responsibility. That's my area of responsibility and every minute we're spending here is time we're not getting the system back up."

Great leaders take more of the blame and less of the credit, and in this instance the department director absorbed the brunt of the more senior manager's frustration. After she was alone again with the new IT employee, she closed her eyes and said, "Don't ever do that again. If you do, we'll have a different kind of conversation."

The new employee felt more than relief. His respect for his department leader exponentially increased, and he became the hardest-working and most loyal employee.

Creating a culture of innovation depends on the extent to which leaders can manage changes, and building the loyalty and trust needed to successfully win the support of team members may happen in one-on-one situations such as the exchange between a director and her IT employee.

> Great leaders take on the blame and pass on the credit to their team. Are you a great leader?

Continuous Improvement

The symbolism of the laurel wreath began in Ancient Greece where victorious athletes were given one to wear on their heads. The laurel was believed to be a sacred plant, declared by the god Apollo, after his true love was turned into a laurel tree in Greek mythology. The laurel wreath was given to winning athletes competing in the Phythian Games beginning around the 6th century BC. The symbolism of the laurel was later adopted by the Olympic games, and later still by the Romans who presented laurel wreaths to military commanders to honor their victories. Today, the laurel wreath is still a symbol of great accomplishment and accolades. Perhaps most famously used to recognize those who have made great contributions to mankind as a Nobel Laureate.

However, after achieving a great victory or accomplishment, some people might tend to "rest on their laurels." This is to say that they become so tied up in their former achievements and glory that they neglect to improve upon them going forward. Neglecting to continuously improve on former successes quickly exposes individuals and organizations to a future of mediocrity.

Change is never done in an organization that understands the need for continuous improvement. People tend to be bothered by things that are not done—everyone loves closure. This tendency can make people uncomfortable with continuous improvement, and this causes organizations to get trapped on autopilot; people would rather do things the way they have always been done than try something new to improve.

Are you a change agent, or someone who is more comfortable with the status quo?

Researchers conducted a study using five monkeys in a habitat. They put a banana at the top of the stairs in the monkey habitat, and when a monkey saw the banana it would run up to the top of the stairs to eat it. A researcher would spray all the monkeys with ice-cold water until the one monkey backed away from the banana.

After some time, the monkeys understood that the banana meant bad. Then they replaced one of the monkeys in the habitat with a new monkey. This new monkey, upon seeing the banana, would start heading up the stairs for the prize. In the study, the other four monkeys grabbed it, thumped it on the head, and dragged it to the bottom of the stairs so that it would not reach the banana and trigger the cold water spray. The newly introduced monkey also developed the view that the banana was not such a good idea. The researchers then replaced another monkey that had been sprayed with ice cold water with a new monkey. When it saw the banana, it started up the stairs and all the monkeys grabbed it and pulled it to the bottom of the steps.

Another monkey was pulled out, and a new one put in its place. As the other had done, it saw the banana and approached the treat. All the monkeys grabbed it, dragged it to the bottom of the stairs—including the two new monkeys who have never been sprayed with water. The researchers repeated this process until they have replaced all five monkeys in the habitat with new monkeys who have never been sprayed with water. Not one of those monkeys would ever go for that banana again—and they had no idea why. All they knew was that avoiding the banana was *just the way they have always done things* in this habitat. They did not question the process. A "just the way we have always done things" attitude plagues many organizations and teams. Leaders who want innovation must take away the sting of the banana and recondition others to see the benefits of new methods.

Never think of improvement as being complete. Changes happen all the time in the business environment: people and organizations require adaptation to remain relevant. But continuous improvement does not mean that your job is to change everything. If you had to change all your habits every day, you would not get through the day! As the leader, your job is to create sustained excellence through continuous, strategic improvement. So, how can you encourage continuous improvement through innovation in your organization? Make sure you encourage innovation, and avoid any barriers to change that you might have encountered from your team. There are three common barriers to innovation that exist in many organizations: the boss, arbitrary rules and regulations, and self-confidence.

The boss (this may be you!) often acts as a barrier to continuous improvement and innovation. This is visible when the boss does not want to take risks or listen to new ideas. It's easy to imagine how managers might wish to safeguard their position or reputation from the risk of implementing changes. But that is inaccurate. Managers unwilling to explore new methods may put their own positions or reputations at risk if things remain static. When managers repeatedly spray cold water on new ideas, they will stop getting new ideas. Employees may simply stop trying to improve on processes and develop a "this is how we have always done it" mindset. A greater risk is that very talented employees might leave in favor of working in an organization where their ideas can thrive.

Arbitrary rules and regulations create barriers to innovation as well. The attitude is, "Well we can't do it that way because we've always done it this way." Or, "The regulators won't let us do this because there are these special rules." Red tape—regulations, policies, and procedures, many of which can be changed because they're within the company's ability to change—usually changes very slowly and often with great resistance. **Consider the arbitrary rules that might be preventing progress from occurring and lead the revision.**

The third barrier, self-confidence, might be surprising to some. Many organizations lack innovation because individual employees lack self-confidence to bring new ideas to their boss. This often happens due to the presence of the other two barriers: because the rules and regulations and because the boss says no too often. Employees may start losing the confidence that can make a difference.

How do you stop this from happening? The biggest secret to encouraging more innovation from your team is to let them try out their ideas. Not just create them, but actually try them. This is called *prototyping*. Prototyping drives innovation. Organizations that prototype more often are far more innovative than those that do not. There are three basic rules of prototyping that will help ensure that you and your team are prototyping improvements that have a real chance to benefit the organization.

Three Rules of Prototyping

1. Start by asking who benefits.
2. Fail early and fail often.
3. Use show and ask rather than show and tell.

The first rule of prototyping is to always start by asking who benefits. If you change these things, which people will benefit? Will it be easier to manufacture, easier to create? Will some of your customers love it? Maybe other customers will hate it? Will all customers like it? From asking the question of who benefits, you might even discover a need to have more than one prototype. Some markets like it this way; other markets like it that way. Ask the question. The second rule of prototyping is expressed with the witty quip, "Fail early and fail often." Although innovative leaders are not cavalier about failure, they do see the advantage of working through prototypes to produce finished concepts that will exactly meet the needs and wants of customers.

A team that designed office space for clients routinely demonstrated the fail-early-and-fail-often mindset. Within 24 hours of getting a new project, they assembled old chairs and old materials to mock up a concept based on the customer's stated desires. In other words, they started playing with ideas as a means to figure out which ideas might work. The design team would bring their customers in several times to look at their ideas to get a sense of what the customer liked and did not like. Building on the feedback and learning from their failures, the team was consistently able to put together beautiful designs that the customers loved.

The third rule of prototyping is to use show and ask rather than show and tell when presenting new ideas. Instead of reacting to prototypes from your team with telling words like, "I like this, but I don't like that. And I like this. I don't like that," ask questions. Train your team to start a demonstration of prototypes by asking probing questions and inviting others to become part of the prototyping team, in effect, by soliciting their ideas.

People naturally stop trying when repeatedly trying turns to failure. Leaders who understand the value of innovation are also responsible for creating ways for teams to taste success often. By acknowledging incremental successes of teams involved in developing new processes, leaders are often more likely to raise the confidence of team members and restore a winning attitude useful to fostering innovation.

Complex Thinking

Over the last decade, many industries across the world have experienced rapid change, and this pace may not slow down anytime in the near future. This presents some challenges to CEOs, specifically to their ability to lead in change and to hire and develop adaptable managers.

Like many companies, in the past Procter & Gamble shrouded its products in secrecy. Sharing trade secrets is not normally considered a way to grow in a proprietary market. But some years ago, Procter & Gamble decided that it needed to stimulate more innovation. The company decided to open up its ideas to a few trusted suppliers and vendors so that they could get ideas and perspectives.

Starting with the Pampers division of the company, Proctor & Gamble invited key suppliers to come in to view the formerly secretive process used to make the Pampers baby diapers. One of the vendors was a company that, among the many things it manufactured, made golf balls. The company had big equipment that would spin rubber around the core to make the balls. When they looked at the process that Procter & Gamble used to make Pampers, they said, "That's almost exactly the way we make golf balls. We could do this for you, and in fact, we could insert at the bottom of the diaper a rubber band so that the diapers would fit more snugly and stay up on the baby."

Innovation was born in that moment. Pampers enjoyed a huge rise in popularity, and they distanced themselves from their competitors.

The environment for conducting business, whether for profit or not for profit and whether private or public, is more complex than in the past. Leaders adept at complex thinking will be more likely to adapt in complex environments. Like the example with Procter & Gamble, organizations with leaders who weigh the costs and benefits of doing things differently than has been done in the past create advantages for their teams to compete.

Do you encourage new ideas and innovation in others?

Innovation is the spark that drives competitive advantage and strategic change. People do not resist all change; they resist change they do not perceive to be beneficial. Foster innovation in your team by being open to new ideas, tolerant of mistakes, ready to explore different ways. There is nothing wrong with change if it is in the right direction.

Core Competency: Fosters Innovation

Identifies, supports, and champions opportunities for change and continuous improvement. Demonstrates flexibility and adaptability in responding to change and ambiguity.

Competency Skills
- **Change Leadership and Management:** Role models and implements new initiatives effectively within teams and organization
- **Continuous Improvement:** Ongoing effort to develop new and better ideas and new ways of solving problems
- **Complex Thinking:** Adapts approach and develops the best solution to difficult issues involving changes in environment or facts

Fosters Innovation Assessment Questions

1. Are you communicating and painting a clear picture of the change and the benefits of the change?
2. How well does your team trust you? How do you know?
3. Great leaders take on the blame and pass on the credit to their team. Are you a great leader?
4. Are you a change agent or someone who is more comfortable with the status quo?
5. Do you encourage new ideas and innovation in others?

The Leader's Toolkit

1. Identify a change that went well. What made this change initiative successful? Now, identify a change in your organization that did not go so well. What were the contributors or learnings from this initiative? For both examples, identify what the key leaders did to support or not support the change.
2. Create a Change Champions group. This is a group of diverse employees from the areas affected by the change. Use this group to obtain input and feedback about the effectiveness of your communication. The members can offer suggestions about the frequency and messaging of your communication.

You may also see this group organically become advocates for the change initiative.

3. Five Stickies

   a. Each group member gets five stickies, or Post-it Notes, and writes one new idea on each of the stickies.

   b. Once members have completed their ideas, divide the group into partners (of two) and direct them to consolidate their ten stickies to five stickies.

   c. Form groups of four and continue the consolidation exercise until you have a manageable number of new ideas to discuss with the large group.

   d. Remember, there are no bad ideas!

   e. Write the outcome of the session on a board where everyone can see it. For example, New Sales Incentive Program.

10

Models Personal Growth

Do managers have hollow bones? This genetic trait would do little to help them in their roles as directors, supervisors, and team leaders. However, hollow bones and fused vertebrae are among the lightweight traits that hummingbirds possess to help in flight.

Hummingbirds provide us with an example of adaptation. Among roughly 10,000 bird species, this tiny bird's genes are expressed in some unique ways: smaller feet; a long, narrow upper beak; a flexible lower beak; the largest brain of all birds in proportion to the size of their body; an untypically large heart; and wings that can do what other birds cannot do. These attributes have evolved to enable hummingbirds to accomplish their hummingbird jobs.

Managers may never be able to fly forward, backward, sideways, and upside down; may never be capable of sipping tree sap; and may never be able to see both in front and to both sides at the same time. Fortunately, although managers might like to see both in front and to both sides, they don't have to. But, they do need to adapt or adopt traits and abilities that will enable them to lead more effectively.

Leadership learning has evolved, and the newest traits or skills needed to survive in today's environment must be developed. A hummingbird eats half its weight every day. The metaphor is relevant for managers. Skilled leaders must consume information daily, but knowing what to consume and how to make adaptations is essential for survival.

Leaders have two responsibilities related to growing themselves: The first is to develop self-awareness to recognize necessary personal improvements and the importance of continuous learning. The second is to demonstrate personal growth and effective self-management of time and energy. The demonstration component is crucial for building teams committed to growth.

Lack of personal growth is equivalent to aerodynamic drag. To overcome the drag, you might need fewer feathers and lighter bones, but managers develop other personal growth traits that can be demonstrated to other team members. You owe it to yourself and your team to show the importance of personal growth as a means to better job performance and fulfillment.

In our world, where 75 percent of people feel disconnected from their jobs, imagine how raising your passion for work and, in turn, influencing others to be more devoted to their own work might increase the productiveness of your team. This passion starts with self-awareness, continuous learning, and management of your personal energy and time.

Self-Awareness

Self-awareness means clearly understanding your emotions, thoughts, motivations, strengths, and development needs. **Self-awareness in personal growth says that before you do, you must be**. You must work on yourself, recommit to yourself, recommit to excellence, recommit to your passion, and be open to discussing with a mentor or adviser what is working and what is not. When you detect that your passion, commitment, or energy wanes, ask yourself, "Am I getting in my own way?"

Is your thinking getting in the way of your performance and success? Self-awareness relates to the tone of the conversations that you have with yourself and your internal response to external interference. People tend to worry and get consumed by a past or future event over which they have no (or little) control, to the point that they cannot concentrate on what is in front of them now—the present. **Recognizing and then reducing your internal interferences will free you to grow, develop, and perform better as a leader.**

Most interference comes from fears. Fear of being judged by others, making a fool of yourself, and being rejected. And most of all, a fear of failing. And because people tend to exaggerate what they are afraid of, they grow their fears rather than controlling them.

> If you knew you could not fail, what would you be doing differently?

Self-evaluation is interesting when you observe Olympic athletes. These athletes are individuals who are performing at the very top of human athletic ability. They all represent the peak of what a human being can accomplish when passion, drive, and performance are focused on a single goal over a long period. Everyone competing on that level is great. They all practice and train many hours each day. They dedicate their lives to the sport, and not one of them makes a habit of eating poorly or skipping practice; otherwise they would not be there. The difference between those who win medals and those who do not comes down to having a winning state of mind. Getting to that state of mind is not a one-time event, it is a process.

The process starts with becoming aware of how you self-sabotage. Mariana was promoted to lead the diversity efforts in a large manufacturing company. In her new role, she would need to attend many conferences and events on behalf of her organization. One evening, she attended a big event with over 500 attendees and was asked to accept an award and say a few words of appreciation. While she was sitting in the audience, thinking through what she was going to say, she suddenly was overwhelmed with negative thoughts. She had not been feeling well earlier in the day and had taken some cold medicine. She had not slept very well the night before because of her sinus cold. She was wearing an awful-looking outfit that did not fit well. And the negative list kept growing. When she heard the name of her company, she proceeded to walk up to the stage and podium. She later could not recall anything beyond the bright lights because of her anxious self-doubt, not even the name of the organization presenting the award. At the podium, she uttered a simple and awkward "thank you" and quickly walked off the stage and out of the auditorium.

Think back to a time when you sabotaged yourself, a time when you got up to the starting line and started thinking, "I didn't sleep enough . . . . I didn't practice enough last week." The process of getting to a winning state of mind is also about understanding your disposition—are you an optimist or are you a pessimist?

When something negative happens or something goes wrong, a pessimist will think, "See? I was right. I knew it would end up like this." Pessimists rationalize, and this affects every aspect of their life. However, when something negative happens, an optimist thinks, "I will learn from this; this is a great lesson. I will be more prepared next time." If something good happens, an optimist may think, "Well, of course, this is what should happen, because I am worthy and a magnet for goodness, and for good things!"

One advantage to being pessimistic is that you are always right. Pessimists have a terrible time on the journey to finding out if they are right. Optimists have a great time finding out whether they are right; and things do not work out 100 percent of the time for optimists, perhaps because they set their goals high. So how do you change? How do you control or manage your self-sabotage or your pessimistic thoughts? How do you focus your mind in a productive, more confident manner? And how do you do this just in time, at the starting line of the big race? **Change is a process, not an event, and it requires daily practice.**

Mariana could have wallowed in her negative feelings after leaving the event. But the next day, she went for a walk and decided that never again would she fall victim to self-sabotage. Mariana may never become the world's best public speaker, but she did become an expert at controlling her negative thoughts. This was a personal breakthrough for Mariana and it started with a strong personal commitment. She created a mantra of "It's show time" to use when she needed to pull her energy forward and be her best. She realized that if she was going to improve, she would need to practice and embrace her fears. Instead of declining invitations to speak, she accepted these invitations to practice and improve. She became very aware when negative thoughts were about to enter, and pushed these thoughts away with a mindful swish and an energetic focus on "It's show time."

> What is your mechanism to control or manage your self-sabotage or pessimistic thoughts?

To manage your thoughts, you must be in a state of focus, a state of single-mindedness. One thought at a time—it is what you think about your thoughts. Mariana was promoted to director the following year, and she believed her promotion largely was due in part to believing in herself and her daily practice of mindfulness. Mariana believed she was already a director. She saw herself as a director-level professional. She did not wait for the promotion, but was daily feeding her mind with the belief. Mariana was committed to her personal development, even though in her advanced role she had many priorities and deadlines. To practice her single-mindedness, she became a **serial single tasker, doing many things but just one at a time**. This involved picking up one thing, but then putting it down before picking up another.

When you are multitasking, you have no power over your thoughts. They are too divided. If you practice living your life one thought at a time, you can manage and focus those thoughts. If you are frequently multitasking, you're allowing your mind to operate on autopilot and possibly diminishing the inspiration that comes from being alert to the details of a single project or initiative. Although you may be at the starting line, if your headspace is negative you will not win that race. Multitasking degrades performance because your mind is processing other thoughts rather than being focused on just one.

Through your daily practice of self-awareness, your goal is to become a focused and mindful being and to develop helpful tools that work best for you. Gather your mind into focus right here, right now. Capture and push away those negative thoughts. **Create in vivid replay of one of your best days or your best experiences**. In great detail, visualize something that you did extremely well. Keep visualizing that success or wonderful experience many times in your head so that you might be in that frame of mind the next time you are challenged.

Close your eyes for a moment and quiet your mind. Think about one specific time when you excelled, when everything worked well. Visualize what you were wearing, the time of the day, where you were, what you said, who you were with. Capture this and name it, then write it down. Name this moment. And next time when you feel the anxiety and fear encroaching, retrieve and relive the moment in your head and bridge back to that time. This psychological exercise, simple as it is, has the potential to calm and provide you with energy for confronting, accepting, and moving forward productively.

Positive affirmation is important because words can have tremendous power over your mind and subsequently your performance. A powerful way to structure your thoughts and transform your goals into results is through self-affirmation. An affirmation is a strong, positive self-statement, spoken in the present tense. It is a preplanned statement of an aspiration, presented to the mind as if it already has been achieved. It may be worthwhile to pause from reading to craft your daily positive affirmation. Write your daily affirmation on a note and post it to your computer screen or set a screensaver to keep the forward-looking message in front of your face. **What is your daily positive affirmation?**

Continuous Learning

As a leader, your commitment to lifelong learning and development is essential to your own success and to modeling behaviors that encourage development on your team and in your organization. Continuous learning involves proactively developing and improving skills and knowledge. Never stop learning and readily volunteer for new projects and challenges.

Debbie, the fourth-generation chief executive officer (CEO) of her family-run electrical services organization, made a significant commitment to continuous learning following her experience participating in leadership development training with her management team. She saw and felt how each training class energized her team to think bigger and innovate processes. They collectively applied many of the tools learned from leadership training, including working more beneficially with dissatisfied customers and running more effective meetings. They began to embrace and learn from their mistakes and apply necessary changes to the business on an ongoing basis rather than simply continuing to do business as usual.

It did not take Debbie long to realize how much this training was improving her business, and how much they had yet to learn. She invested in constructing a 1,200-square-foot on-site training facility where they could train more often and hold a greater variety of training classes. Now they hold their leadership training classes in their new facility and they invite others to join technical training classes where technicians can get certified.

The new site cost Debbie's organization about $40,000, but has since paid for itself. Her employee retention has improved dramatically, and the new ideas, skills, and competencies that come from employees who are trained and knowledgeable in various areas of the business has been greatly rewarding for the organization. Through her team's hard work, she has seen her organization grow from a moderately successful company for 33 years to one that is highly successful and has become a market leader in the region.

A best practice for leaders to anchor their learning is to teach others. At a bank headquartered in Vietnam with operations throughout Southeast Asia, there is not just one leader, manager, or employee who has a leadership training success story, but many. The bank enrolled 15 managers and leaders—including the CEO—in a live and interactive leadership training program. Participating in these programs inspired them to create a culture of learning within the bank organization. Each top manager is now responsible to teach the leadership topics they have learned during their classes to their employees. Once a month, they facilitate a leadership development activity internally for their staff, passing along insights and ideas that have created lasting improvements.

This has had a significant impact on the bank's bottom line, particularly for its long-term development. Management has observed that they have created an entirely new culture within the organization. Communications within and between departments are far more open and effective; employees are passionate and engaged; customer satisfaction has greatly improved; and the bank has experienced significant savings through greater operational efficiencies.

Perhaps the most rewarding thing you can do as a leader is to share your knowledge and experience with others. While you continue your leadership development journey, keep others in mind. Remember, **school is never out for the pro**. There is always something new for you to learn, or something timeless for you to pass on to others on your team or in your organization.

Leaders who hope to generate enthusiasm for learning new things must model great performance and continuous improvement daily. If you want your employees to be more passionate about their jobs, demonstrate your passion for your job, even on tough, stressful days.

Many misunderstand passion. People say that all that's required to be successful is passion—passion for what you do. Passion is what distinguishes remarkable performance and growth from the ordinary. But a problem may occur when leaders are not passionate about their own work or the example they set. There are four sources of passion, so if you're not passionate about (1) what you do, then find your passion by focusing on (2) how you do it, (3) why you do it, or (4) who you do it for or with.

Lack of passion should not excuse poor performance. Outstanding leaders do their best whether they feel like it or not, and they do that because of discipline.

To develop as a great leader, first understand why you work and then the strengths that you bring to your role. Leaders role model discipline and positive attitude. They continuously look for ways to improve their own performance, not continuing to do the same things in the same way when there may be a better way. **Great leaders strive for stair-step development,** not incremental development. Stair-step development requires significant commitment to personal growth and impact. It requires the leader to take on a new role, or new projects that require new skills. It may involve a cross-functional move into another area within your organization. These great leaders strive for improvement and change. They gain clarity through self-assessment and feedback from others on areas they must improve, and they develop a plan. They are in action.

A development plan outlines development objectives and defines how feedback and progress will be measured. A leader committed to personal growth will own his or her development plan and ensure it is measurable. Being closed to feedback is being closed to development. Think of feedback as a gift, not as a negative. Real development is not a one-time event, it is not about merely attending a conference, reading, or watching a video. Creating new experiences for yourself and for members of your team is a solid stepping-stone to growth.

> Are you continually growing yourself as a leader? What is your personal development plan?

Managing Personal Energy and Time

To be an effective role model, take care of yourself. You cannot take care of other people if you do not take care of yourself. Leading people, building teams, and role modeling is hard work and requires extraordinary effort and energy. Find ways to fuel your personal energy and manage your time.

> Purpose is our directional magnet and life fuel. It is aspirational and frustrating, and disciplined leaders who intentionally grow themselves actualize their potential.

Managing Personal Energy

A key element to personal energy is having a purpose. As you progress in your career to lead larger teams and deal with more complex issues, you will regularly face conflicts and negative issues. Having a mechanism to aid in your daily maneuvering is key to enjoying the journey. Recommit to your purpose and do not allow small obstacles or negatives to pull you off course. Do not ignore these

---

issues, but do put them into perspective without allowing them to zap your energy.

One manager on the senior administrative staff at a pediatric hospital described a pattern in his personal life to reinvigorate his mind and attitude following particularly draining periods of work. "I stay grounded in my professional life by doing meaningful things outside of work." He added, "But there are times when I feel like the Phoenix." The Phoenix, as other similar mythological birds like the Fêng-Huang, the Benu, or the Firebird, burns down to ashes before being reborn. Leadership can be exhausting, and when managers feel burned out, they need to rejuvenate to return to life, so to speak. But avoiding burnout is better. Create daily rituals that constantly remind you of your purpose and passion, and pause long enough to replace negative thoughts with hopeful ones. Briefly stepping outside of the rush of activity might allow leaders to put problems in perspective. The next step is to help others do the same.

Exercise is also proven to help leaders manage personal energy. Just 20 minutes of cardiovascular exercise 3 days a week will markedly improve your energy and stamina. Most leaders and managers are doing less physically demanding work but more mentally demanding work. This bulk of mental work can leave you feeling fatigued. Although scientists have found no biological correlation between brain activity and physical response to activity,[8] managers often claim to feel more physically fatigued after a full day of high mental focus. The physical side effects of mental fatigue might include irritability, sleep loss, and diminished focus. Physical exercise counteracts this unbalance and actually improves feelings of fatigue.[9]

Exercise may be the best cure for fatigue. Do you make time for at least 20 minutes of exercise three days a week?

Refill your personal energy tank. It is best if you practice this all the time, steadily, rather than waiting until you are running on empty. There are two key re-energizers to fill up your tank: inspiration and humor. Expose yourself to as many positive thoughts and laugh as often as you can every day. **Take your job seriously but take yourself lightly.** Laughing is most often seen as the objective for comedians but not for organization leaders. Making humor work in business can break stress cycles and help people feel better. When you bring people joy, they want to work with you, and they are more likely to give the service quality you want. Of course, good judgment matters. Laughing at other people is not a good relationship investment. Laughing with people can build rapport and teamwork.

Also, take time to empty your mind; most people typically think of this in the form of meditation or prayer. Tuck yourself away and clear your mind to renew your resilience. If you are not in the practice of doing this already and see the potential value, you might start with just 2 to 3 minutes each morning, move to 5, then 10, then perhaps 20 or 30 to devote to fixing your headspace.

Vicente, a manager for a laboratory testing organization based in Chile, had been miserable for almost 2 years. On top of his stressful job, he had a family to provide for and two ailing parents who he and his wife were taking care of. His stress levels had become so high that he was on a prescription regime to manage it. The medication had adverse side effects: they often made him feel dizzy and slowed down his reaction time. Vicente felt as though he was living in a blur, and the effect was only worsening his ability to manage others.

During one of his leadership training sessions, Vicente learned about stress management in a way he had never previously considered, and it completely changed his perspective. By addressing daily meditation and breathing exercises as part of his daily to-do list, he little by little stopped needing stress medications. Every morning, he took a few minutes before departing his home for work to sit quietly and breathe deeply and slowly. As he began to feel more in control and able to manage his team and his career, Vincente increased the time spent meditatively early each morning. Separating your work life from life outside of work may be less effective than committing to a holistic approach to balance your mind and body. **To lead others, you must first lead yourself; and to lead yourself, you must take care of yourself.**

Managing Personal Time

The ability to manage personal energy requires effectively managing time. Have you ever heard the expression: "If you want to get something done, ask a busy person to do it"? Some people seem to have a special ability to accomplish far more than others in the same amount of time. It is as if they have 70 minutes in each hour. Most people think the smart ones will be able to be productive and accomplish great things with their time, but it is not the acquisition of knowledge that allows people to make the most of their time; rather, it is the application of knowledge that results in greater productivity. There are simple actions you might take that will allow you to manage time better.

"I do not have enough time." That feeling that you will never get everything on your project list done generally causes managers to be less productive. An ordinary pitcher and a glass can provide an illuminating visual lesson. The pitcher represents those things that you want to get done and the glass is your day. You may think about all the things that you want to get accomplished and then look at the amount of time available to do it. Managers with many duties often say, "There is no way I'm going to get all of this done today." And you keep on telling yourself that throughout the day. Is it any wonder that a manager who thinks this way ends the day frustrated and disappointed, perhaps even defeated?

Many people spend time on the easy and unimportant things, and that generally interferes with accomplishing the most important priorities. The habit of great leaders is to focus on what's most important without feeling overwhelmed and frustrated by endless things to accomplish. Focus on your most valuable and profitable activities (MVPs).

Focusing on your MVPs takes effort and commitment. What are the six to eight activities that are the most valuable and profitable to your department or organization, or that generate the biggest return on your investment of time and talent? Recognizing the MVPs can be a deliberate process that involves monitoring the way you spend your time. But after determining the activities that consistently produce the greatest impact, primarily do those things. Once you are clear about the priorities, spend at least 60 percent of your time every day doing them. This is rarely easy! Crises, interruptions, urgent issues, and emergencies are going to happen, so it is unfair to yourself and your team to expect you to focus on your MVPs 100 percent of the time. However, focusing on your MVPs 60 percent to 80 percent of every day will produce astounding results. Activity can be the anesthesia for ineffective leadership. What do you accomplish with your time and energy? One of the great paradoxes is that to the degree we become focused, we can do less and accomplish more. That is because focusing on what produces results produces the right activity.

To-Do List Failure

How often do you have problems managing your time from your to-do list? Imagine this scenario. Assume you have included 20 things on your list, and by noon you have completed several things. You are feeling pretty good, but your lunch starts to settle in and your energy level begins to wane as you hit the afternoon slump. Now it is an hour until you are supposed to be done for the day but, in fact, the five most important activities of your day have not been completed!

Prioritizing is necessary to accomplishing more with your time. Crossing off things from your to-do list often feels like accomplishment. But it is not bottom-line accomplishment. To significantly improve your rate of success, concentrate on the things that are most important, not the things that are easiest to cross off your list. Leadership includes the role of coach, and training the members of your team to focus on MVP activities can dramatically boost productivity. You might individually ask them to share with you what they believe are their six to eight priority activities and engage them in a discussion so that you both can agree on the MVPs.

Lack-of-Time Analysis

Think about how you spend 100 percent of your time at work. The habit of good time management depends on how well you know the major functions of things that you must do and have estimated the amount of time spent on each. How accurate is your estimate?

Using little leadership tools can produce big results. Begin to analyze how you use your time by completing a job function analysis. This analysis basically describes the major activities of your job but also the typical things that you might spend time doing. Divide them the way you think is most appropriate to analyze and then attach percentages to each thing totaling 100 percent of your available time. Managers who keep track using a detailed time log can create an accurate picture of behaviors. A simple self-study might span a week, once a year, and so on. Every time you change activities, log it. At the end of your tracking period, look at the activities you are doing versus the ones you had planned to do. The truth may be surprising. Managers who have done this exercise have concluded they were spending too much time on less important activities.

Lack of Scheduling Technique

James McCay, author of *The Management of Time*, wrote, "**Nothing ever happens until you create a space for it to happen in.**"[10] Scheduling involves more than meetings. Blocking time on your calendar for thinking, writing, calling, and doing enables you to reserve time on your schedule for specific activities other than meetings. Committing to do specific things, you may quickly discover that less important things have been a distraction in the past. The same disciplined approach to managing time applies to social media and email as well as time spent socializing with others in your workspace.

Doing Nonessentials

Stop doing some of the things that you are doing so that you have more time to do other more important and profitable things. Chinese philosopher, Ling Utang, taught, "Besides the noble art of getting things done, there is the noble art of leaving things undone." He also said, "The wisdom of life consists in the elimination of nonessentials." A study that monitored the time use of top executives in Fortune 500 companies worldwide discovered a single characteristic in every top executive: each had the propensity to eliminate nonessentials from their life. Now, that's a good philosophy, but how is it done?

Consider three different ways to eliminate nonessentials. The first is to understand the 80/20 rule. The 80/20 rule is the idea that in any group of items there is a small percentage of items, about 20 percent, which account for 80 percent of the value. The other 80 percent of the items account for only 20 percent of the value. The implication for leaders is that achieving better results faster starts with not doing 80 percent of the stuff that ends up on your to-do list. Focus instead on the 20 percent that generates the highest value.

The second way to eliminate nonessentials is to think about the perfectionist principle. Perfectionism is detrimental to time management, because it puts too much of the focus on getting something done perfectly rather than punctually. This derives from Parkinson's Law, which says that work will tend to expand to the time available for its completion. Perfectionists may think that something has to be perfect, so they overinflate the amount of time needed to get it done. If you're a perfectionist, simply do your work in half the time you think you need. Whatever time it normally takes you, just force yourself into doing it in half the time.

The final way to eliminate nonessentials is through the Important–Urgent Matrix. The tool is a simple square divided into four quadrants. In the upper left quadrant (category 1), write those tasks that are truly both important and urgent. In the upper right quadrant (category 2), write those tasks that are important but less urgent. The other two quadrants are true time stealers. Tasks in the bottom left quadrant (category 3) are not important but, for whatever reason, are very urgent. And tasks in the bottom right quadrant (category 4) are neither urgent nor important. You should not spend any of your time on tasks in category 4 by either delegating these tasks or removing them from the list altogether. Everything falls into one of these four categories. There are things that are important and urgent and those that are not. Analyze your activities and then try to increase the time that you spend in category 2—important but not yet urgent—by eliminating time that you spend in category 3, where less important things appear to take priority.

> Are you spending your time on the most important elements of your life (personal and professional)?

There are many things that distract from efficient use of time. "Distract" is only one word that describes a loss of control of your own calendar and commitments. Some things hijack your time. Some less important activities even hold managers hostage. Instead of allowing the activities of the day to distract you from the most important business or seduce you to waste time, develop the time-controlling habits of exceptional leaders and then mentor the members of your team to do the same.

The hummingbird metaphor at the beginning of this chapter describes traits that hummingbirds have that help in flight. The greatest trait that helps leaders to fly, in a manner of speaking, is personal growth. Self-awareness, commitment to continuous learning, and tightly managing time and energy are the defining behaviors that leaders should model for everyone on their teams. Modeling personal growth is the secret of durable leadership.

Core Competency: Models Personal Growth

Maintains an attitude of open, curious, and proactive learning—continually expanding own area of understanding and expertise. Demonstrates awareness and accurate assessment of personal effectiveness, and practices methods to maintain and generate positive energy through stressful situations.

Competency Skills
- **Self-Awareness:** Clearly understands one's emotions, thoughts, motivations, strengths, and development needs
- **Continuous Learning:** Proactively develops and improves skills and knowledge, never stops learning, and readily volunteers for new projects and challenges
- **Managing Personal Energy and Time:** Establishes rituals and responses to manage personal energy, enabling a greater presence and focus

Models Personal Growth Assessment Questions

1. If you knew you could not fail, what would you be doing differently?
2. What is your mechanism to control or manage your self-sabotage or pessimistic thoughts?
3. Are you continually growing yourself as a leader? What is your personal development plan?
4. Exercise may be the best cure for fatigue. Do you make time for at least 20 minutes of exercise three days a week?
5. Are you spending your time on the most important elements of your life (personal and professional)?

The Leader's Toolkit

1. Leaders and teams need to feel like they have a win, which helps to fuel personal energy. Sometimes, when there are so many conflicting priorities, you do not feel like you are winning or getting anything accomplished. This affects your engagement and energy. Try this exercise to help provide focus and alignment within the team:

a. Gather your team together first thing in the morning on Monday on a weekly basis.

b. Have each team member bring the most important project or task he or she must accomplish that week. Each member can only submit one item. (Although we all know that we all have more than one thing we will accomplish during the week, the exercise is meant to bring focus to the most important task.)

c. Assign a scribe and ensure the scribe notes the name, week, and task that each team member submits for the week.

d. The following Monday, have each person report on his or her actions and then commit to the current week's actions.

e. At the end of the team reports, take a couple of minutes to say a few words about the upcoming week—words of appreciation for the hard work, focus, and energy for the upcoming week.

2. Breathe to Calm. Commit to this exercise for at least one week and assess how you feel.

a. Two to three times per day

b. Find a quiet place, with no cellphone or other distractions.

c. Close your eyes.

d. Take ten deep breaths: inhale slowly and deeply, then slowly exhale.

Focus only on the elements of your breathing.

CONCLUSION

Make Leadership a Habit

C restcom International makes the world a better place by developing stronger, more ethical leaders around the world. Ethical leaders take responsibility for both good and bad results, and those who learn and consistently do the recommendations in this book are more likely than others to create a workforce committed to achieving the purpose and vision of their leaders and their organizations. They are more likely to make better decisions and have lasting impact.

The stories and scenarios shared in this book have illustrated how the transformation of managers, supervisors, directors, and team leaders, wherever they are in the world, is due to training and consistent activities that drive results. These individuals follow the habits of great leaders.

The introduction to the book described leadership as a language that can be learned. The language of leaders is not limited to words but instead to the way leaders communicate through actions. No matter where Crestcom clients and alumni are in the world, we all now speak a common language built around achieving results, building teams, influencing, business acumen, vision, excellence, relationships, customers, innovation, and growth. Learning any language requires practice and starts with a good teacher or context for understanding. Leadership is what binds us, moves us, and challenges us to continually take action to becoming even better leaders. Managers who want to achieve more every year must get better every year.

How do you put together training that will successfully change behavior? There are three fundamentals that you must include to change behavior through training. The first fundamental is measured development, and this principle can be applied to reading this book. Start with one thing. Make each new skill part of your management behavior before you tackle the next. The second fundamental is to have an implementation plan. Design a goal and measurable steps to improve in one specific area. Then do it. Specify *what* you've learned, *when* you are planning to implement it, and *how* you are planning to measure the results. The third fundamental is accountability. Hold yourself accountable to complete your personal improvement plans. Great leaders set their own bar; they role model accountability and continuous growth and perspective.

In our 30 years of leadership training, we became convinced there was a missing link in the training and development of managers. The way we addressed that at Crestcom is by partnering with top trainers who we identified worldwide in each skill area. More than 25 subject matter experts have joined our faculty and participate with us in designing training content and media that we apply to the fundamentals in our hands-on, interactive training sessions to change behaviors and develop leaders.

Treating the 30 skills in the book as a set of accessible tools equips you to deal appropriately, even advantageously, with every sort of leadership and management issue that arises. Recognizing the best tool in each situation requires familiarity and practice. Be clear about the Afters each time you set a goal to improve your leadership. In other words, what do you expect will happen after you've accomplished your goal to master a new skill? The steps you may take to achieve goals with clear Afters are typically more specific and focused.

You are a role model, and your decisions and actions have an impact on your team, your organization, and your community. It is your duty to yourself and your team to commit to developing your leadership habit. You have not started on a leadership journey to simply go through the motions, making occasional changes. Instead, have an impact. Struggle, and through that struggle you will grow day after day, month after month, and year after year. Never stop growing, and be genuinely curious.

As you gather knowledge and experiences that allow you to grow in your leadership, share the value of your learning with others. Sharing your knowledge, insights, and perspectives has a multiplier effect that may allow others at times to improve without struggling. As they share with others in turn, this abundance of knowledge and experiences collectively builds a global network of better leaders.

The Leadership Habit communicates 10 core leadership competencies and 30 essential skills that can transform behaviors to drive results. Make leadership your habit.

REFERENCES

1. RANDALL BECK and JIM HARTER, "Why Great Managers Are So Rare." *Gallup Business Journal*, March 25, 2014, accessed October 12, 2016, www.gallup.com/businessjournal/167975/why-great-managers-rare.aspx
2. "The Emperor's Mighty Brother." *The Economist*, December 19, 2015, accessed October 31, 2016, www.economist.com/news/christmas-specials/21683980-demand-aphrodisiac-has-brought-unprecedented-wealth-rural-tibetand-trouble
3. WERNER von SIEMENS, Siemens Corporate Archives 2007, accessed November 01, 2016, www.siemens.com/history/pool/perseunlichkeiten/gruendergeneration/werner_von_siemens_en.pdf
4. "SpaceX Careers." n.d., accessed November 02, 2016, www.spacex.com/careers
5. KYLE W. LUTHANS, "Recognition: A Powerful, but often Overlooked, Leadership Tool to Improve Employee Performance." *Journal of Leadership & Organizational Studies*, January 01, 2000, 7 (1), 31–39, accessed August 01, 2016, www.researchgate.net/publication/250961590_Recognition_A_Powerful_but_often_Overlooked_Leadership_Tool_to_Improve_Employee_Performance, doi: 10.1177/107179190000700104
6. Bureau of Labor Statistics, U.S. Department of Labor, "Lost-Worktime Injuries and Illnesses: Characteristics and Resulting Days Away From Work, 2001," March 27, 2003, accessed September 7, 2016, //www.bls.gov/news.release/history/osh2_03272003.txt
7. ESTEBAN KOLSKY, "CX for Executives," September 3, 2015, accessed August 12, 2016, www.slideshare.net/ekolsky/cx-for-executives
8. DANIEL ENGBER, "FYI: Does Thinking Too Hard Wear You Out?" *Popular Science*, March 1, 2013, accessed November 1, 2016, www.popsci.com/science/article/2013–02/fyidoes-thinking-too-hard-wear-you-out

9. TARA PARKER-POPE, "The Cure for Exhaustion? More Exercise." *New York Times*, February 29, 2008, retrieved November 01, 2016, http://well.blogs.nytimes.com/2008/02/29/the-cure-for-exhaustion-more-exercise/
10. JAMES T. MCCAY, *The Management of Time*. Englewood Cliffs, NJ: Prentice-Hall 1959.

APPENDIX A

Your Personal Development Plan

Crestcom's leadership development program involves the creation of personal action plans that are followed up with accountability coaching sessions. We do this to ensure that our clients are not simply learning leadership skills but are internalizing them and applying them to create impact for their organization. In this spirit, we wanted to close this book with a Personal Development Plan. Take about 10 minutes to fill out this Personal Development Plan for yourself, and then hold yourself accountable to it. Perhaps make a copy and give it to your boss, team, spouse, or friend and ask him or her to remind you of your plan. If you find that you need more, perhaps more perspective from other leaders in your area; more content to understand the competencies; or more accountability to apply the knowledge, tools, and techniques outlined in this book, reach out to us. We would be happy to connect you with a group of other leaders in your local community who have made their own commitment to their leadership development journey.

Step 1: Self-Assessment

Rate yourself on a scale from 1 to 10 on your skill level for each of the 10 core leadership competencies. A score of 1 means it is an area of opportunity for you to improve in, whereas a 10 means that you are very strong in this core competency.

Drives for Results	Encourages Excellence
• Accountability • Decision Making • Asking the Right Questions	• Delegation and Empowerment • Coaching and Encouraging • Rewards and Recognition
Builds the Right Team	**Develops Positive Relationships**
• Hiring the Right Talent • Multigenerational Leadership • Organizing and Developing Teams	• Collaboration • Networking • Conflict Management
Influences Others	**Develops Customer Focus**
• Open and Effective Communication • Negotiation and Building Consensus • Emotional Intelligence	• Trust and Credibility • Responsive Problem Solving • Needs and Opportunity Awareness
Understands the Business	**Fosters Innovation**
• Generates Business Insights • Financial Management • Productivity and Process Efficiency	• Change Leadership and Management • Continuous Improvement • Complex Thinking

Executes Vision	Models Personal Growth
• Defines and Communicates Vision • Strategic Thinking • Plans and Prioritizes	• Self-Awareness • Continuous Learning • Managing Personal Energy and Time

Total Score:

Pick one competency that you have identified that is an opportunity for improvement, and pick one that is a strength you can leverage. These two competencies go into your Action Plan.

Step 2: Personal Action Plan

Strength Competency

Name: _____

Company: _____

Date: _____

Strength Competency: _____

What is your goal to leverage your strength competency? Be specific.

_____
_____
_____
_____
_____

What current organizational challenge or opportunity will achieving this goal address?

_____
_____
_____
_____
_____

Specify at least three actions you will take to accomplish this goal.

1. _____
   _____

2. _____
   _____

3. _____
   _____

4. _____
   _____

When will you start?

_____
_____
_____
_____
_____

When will this plan be accomplished?

_____
_____
_____
_____
_____

How will you know that you have achieved your goal (what does success look like)? Write a qualitative description.

_____
_____
_____
_____
_____

How will you measure achieving your goal?

_____
_____
_____
_____
_____

Improvement Competency

Name: _____

Company: _____

Date: _____

Strength Competency: _____

What is your goal to improve on your opportunity for growth competency? Be specific.

_____
_____
_____
_____
_____

What current organizational challenge or opportunity will achieving this goal address?

_____
_____
_____
_____
_____

Specify at least three actions you will take to accomplish this goal.

1. _____
   _____
2. _____
   _____
3. _____
   _____
4. _____
   _____

When will you start?

_____
_____
_____
_____

When will this plan be accomplished?

_____

_____

_____

_____

_____

How will you know that you have achieved your goal (what does success look like)? Write a qualitative description.

_____

_____

_____

_____

_____

How will you measure achieving your goal?

_____

_____

_____

_____

_____

Step 3: Accountability

How will you hold yourself accountable for achieving your Personal Development Plan?

_____

_____

_____

_____

_____

Sign up for a 360 Degree Feedback Assessment by contacting your local Crestcom training facilitator at http://www.crestcomleadership.com/find-local -training/.

APPENDIX B

Core Competencies Summary

Chapter 1: Drives for Results

Core Competency: Drives for Results

Focuses on what is important and creates a sense of urgency, successfully managing multiple priorities. Implements tracking and follow-up mechanisms to ensure rapid progress. Identifies and understands issues and takes action that is consistent with available facts and risk.

Competency Skills
- *Accountability:* Establishes clear responsibilities and processes for monitoring, communicating progress, and measuring results
- *Decision Making:* Uses the information available and best judgment to make a timely decision
- *Asking the Right Questions:* Probes the thought process of others and asks the right questions to uncover root causes to problems and better solutions

---

Drives for Results Assessment Questions

1. Do your employees own the results of the projects and initiatives assigned to them? Do they own and drive for results, or do they merely go through the motion of effort?

2. What is your tracking mechanism for your department's goals?

3. How do you ensure accountability? Start by answering these questions. Do all projects and initiatives have:

   a. A goal—what does winning look like?

   b. One clear owner?

   c. A project plan with dates, deliverables, and a point person for each deliverable?

   d. A standard check-in process for deliverables?

4. When starting a new project, do you take the time to slow down to speed up?

5. Are you asking probing questions to understand future needs?

The Leader's Toolkit

1. Are you accountable to organizational values when you decide on actions that affect others?

   a. List the stated values of your organization.

   b. Describe in writing how each value should influence decisions made on your team or by you or someone in your organization.

   The Afters of this simple exercise are to always drive decisions based on holding yourself accountable to the values you claim as an organization.

2. Are you asking the right questions? Create a list of five future-based questions that you could ask yourself or others to ensure an accurate understanding of the underlying purpose of any project.

Chapter 2: Builds the Right Team

Core Competency: Builds the Right Team

Attracts, selects, and forms teams with diverse styles and perspectives. Fosters productive and collaborative teamwork and a sense of belonging for team members.

Competency Skills
- *Hiring the Right Talent:* Attracts and selects high-caliber talent to best meet the needs of the organization
- *Multigenerational Leadership:* Understands and values the importance of a generationally diverse workforce with different perspectives and working styles
- *Organizing and Developing Teams:* Establishes common goals and creates a collaborate sense of belonging team environment

---

Builds the Right Team Assessment Questions

1. What is your process for selecting the right talent for your team?
2. What is your process for onboarding talent? Do your team members understand your expectations and how to thrive as a member of your team?
3. How are you leveraging the strengths of all the generations in your organization?
4. How are you recognizing your team's success? Is everyone proud to be a member of your team?

The Leader's Toolkit

1. For your next open position, create a What Great Looks Like description. Think about the person who excels or has excelled in this role; this makes it real. Why is the person great? What are his or her strengths and experiences? Prioritize the behavior competencies given this profile. From this description, develop your job requirements and your interview questions. Ensure that your interview questions are aligned with the behavior competencies and are worded in an action oriented/results format. For example, assume Results Orientation is a key behavior competency required for this position. Here are a few questions you may want to consider in your interview process:

    a. Tell us about the process that you have used to establish goals for your area. What were the process and steps you took? Were you satisfied with the outcome? Why or why not? What were your goals last year?

    b. Tell us about a goal that you set that you did not reach. What obstacles did you encounter?

2. Hold a team retreat and define a team charter. This charter would include:

    a. Purpose: What is the purpose of this team? How does this team add value to the organization?

    b. Communication: How often does the team meet? Channel of communication?

    c. Conflict Resolution: How does the team resolve conflicts?

    d. Quality: How does the team measure quality?

Ensure that the team members get to know each other and understand each other's working style and strengths. Develop a team identity, celebrate wins, and solve issues together. Ensure that everyone on the team has a voice and feel valued.

Chapter 3: Influences Others

Core Competency: Influences Others

Listens and fosters open communication through questioning, dialogue, and information-sharing. Advocates ideas and effectively negotiates to achieve mutually successful outcomes. Identifies and proactively manages own emotions.

Competency Skills
- *Open and Effective Communication:* Listens and fosters open communication through questioning, dialogue, and information-sharing
- *Negotiation and Building Consensus:* Advocates ideas and effectively negotiates to achieve mutually successful outcomes
- *Emotional Intelligence:* Builds productive relationships by managing emotions and practices social awareness of other's emotions

---

Influences Others Assessment Questions

1. During your one-on-one sessions with your employees, do you often talk more than listen?
2. If you lost your title of authority, would you still be effective in influencing other team members?
3. Do you negotiate to win, or do you use your process to strengthen relationships in which both parties feel valued and both win?
4. Is emotional intelligence your soft edge—do you build productive relationships by leveraging your emotional intelligence?

The Leader's Toolkit

1. During your next team meeting, use the $\frac{1}{3}$ +1 Method. Obtain feedback from your team members about how they felt about the process and the meeting. Did they feel their voices were heard?

The $\frac{1}{3}$ + 1 Method

Step 1: Green Light Thinking.

Step 2: Create a list of Coffee Stains.

Step 3: Add up number of Coffee Stains, divide by 3, and then add 1.

Step 4: Vote based on the product of step 3.

Step 5: Tally the votes.

---

2. During your next one-on-one session with your employees, practice asking questions versus telling. In fact, try to *only* ask questions and assess your results.
3. When employees are looking to you to solve an issue for them, first ask:
   a. What is your recommendation?
   b. What have you tried so far?

Through these questions, help them realize that they likely have already solved their own issue. Use this same approach in peer meetings and assess your effectiveness. You may find that the more questions you ask, the more influential you are. Remain genuinely curious.

Chapter 4: Understands the Business

Core Competency: Understands the Business

Understands how businesses and organizations work. Applies knowledge of business drivers, financial indicators, and technology to generate productivity and insights.

Competency Skills
- *Generates Business Insights:* Uses knowledge of business drivers, trends, and how organizations make money to guide actions and generate insights
- *Financial Management:* Uses financial indicators and analysis to evaluate options and proactively manage financial results
- *Productivity and Process Efficiency:* Recognizes synergies and processes in need of improvement and makes suggestions to address problems

---

Understands the Business Assessment Questions

1. Do your employees understand how they affect the business and how they create business value?
2. Are your performance goals for your employees tangible and measurable, and do they tie to the organization's key drivers?
3. What are the most significant external factors affecting your business?
4. Do you ask the bigger questions of your employees about the business?
5. Are you encouraging and allowing your employees to be innovative and curious?
6. What global trends will affect your organization, and how will you navigate or leverage?
7. How effective and efficient are the key business processes in your area?

The Leader's Toolkit

1. Select members of your team to research current trends that affect your organization or department. Have these individuals present their findings to the large group and facilitate discussion around the trends in terms of their potential impact. Here is the recommended facilitation:

a. Present an overview of the key trends to the large group.

b. Split the group up into two groups for discussion and have each group select a facilitator and a scribe.

c. Group 1 discusses: How could this trend positively affect our business? To what degree (1–10 high) could this trend affect our business positively? What action(s) do we recommend to leverage this trend?

d. Group 2 discusses: How could this trend negatively affect our business? To what degree (1–10 high) could this trend affect our business negatively? What action(s) do we recommend to mitigate the possible negative impacts of this trend?

e. Have each group present to one another and together determine what further actions (if any) should occur.

2. Review the glossary list of financial terms in Appendix C with your team, and assign a few key terms to each person (or groups of people for larger teams). At your next team meeting, have each of them present the term and how it specifically applies to your organization. You also may want to invite someone from the finance or accounting department to one of your team meetings to help educate your team on the basic financial terms and how they apply to your organization.

Chapter 5: Executes Vision

Core Competency: Executes Vision

Considers a broad range of internal and external factors when creating strategies and implementing plans. Translates business vision and strategy into plans and sequenced priorities to best deliver results and leverage resources.

Competency Skills

- *Defines and Communicates Vision:* Communicates a compelling picture of the future that connects and motivates others to action

- *Strategic Thinking:* Sees the big picture of future possibility and creates strategic connections leading to competitive advantage

- *Plans and Prioritizes:* Formulates objectives and priorities, implements and monitors plans in alignment with the long-term strategy of the organization

---

Executes Vision Assessment Questions

1. Can your team members repeat your vision to others with clarity and passion?
2. Do you have a group of advisers that can provide different perspectives in your strategic thinking?
3. How often do you monitor your plans and key initiatives?

The Leader's Toolkit

To get your team thinking about vision and communicating a compelling picture of the future, facilitate the following exercise:

1. Assign small groups (no more than six members to each group) and have each group select a facilitator.
2. Task each group to develop an aspirational headline and visual cover story about your organization ten years in the future.
3. Allow for a few minutes of individual thinking time, and then the group facilitator selects a person to start the story.
4. The story continues to build as it moves around the group and each member adds specifics to the story.

Once this warm-up exercise is complete, each group completes a large poster to visually represent the story. This can be done using flipcharts, whiteboards, or poster board. Each group member adds key elements to the poster (e.g., quotes, images, facts).

1. Once complete, the groups review their vision storyboard and create a headline that they write on the top of their poster.
2. Each group presents to the large group, and the other groups provide comments on what they like about each of the presentations.

Chapter 6: Encourages Excellence

Core Competency: Encourages Excellence

Empowers and motivates team members to achieve and creates a feeling of personal investment and desire to excel. Appropriately recognizes the contributions of individuals and teams. Nurtures the development of others through effective coaching and mentoring.

(Continued)

Competency Skills

- *Delegation and Empowerment:* Establishes clear performance goals that encourage others to personally connect to their job

- *Coaching and Encouraging:* Develops others by providing clear feedback on performance and offering positive coaching advice and opportunities to develop skills

- *Rewards and Recognition:* Provides specific, meaningful and timely recognition to individuals and teams for their results

---

Encourages Excellence Assessment Questions

1. Do you understand what motivates each one of your team members?

2. Do you clearly delegate responsibility and authority?

3. How often do your employees receive feedback on what they are doing well and what they need to improve?

4. Have you created a dependent or independent workforce?

5. How many people did you recognize last week?

The Leader's Toolkit

1. Order personalized notecards and create a habit of writing short personal notes to your employees to specifically thank them for their hard work and excellence. You may even see your notecards posted in your employees' offices or cubicles. A thank-you note goes a long way toward letting your employees know you appreciate and value them.

2. Set up standard one-on-one sessions with each of your employees. Ensure that you do not cancel or move these sessions and communicate your preparation expectations. Here is a recommended process for your one-on-one sessions:

   a. A general check-in of how they are doing overall

   b. Actions and progress from prior meeting

   c. Key accomplishments

   d. Feedback: First ask for their feedback on how they feel about their progress, what they have learned, and what they would improve to date. Then, provide your feedback and observations with specifics of what they did well and what they need to improve.

e. Ask, "What do I need to know about?" Here, you are looking for key things that have occurred or may be occurring in the near future.

f. Ask, "What help do you need from me?"

g. Decide on action items from current meeting.

Chapter 7: Develops Positive Relationships

Core Competency: Develops Positive Relationships

Builds partnerships and effective working relationships to meet shared objectives. Recognizes and shows respect for people, ideas, and perspectives that differ from self. Actively seeks to positively resolve interpersonal disagreement and conflict.

Competency Skills

- *Collaboration:* Builds partnerships and works collaboratively with others to achieve shared objectives
- *Networking:* Establishes relationship networks and alliances inside and outside of organization
- *Conflict Management:* Encourages differences of opinions. Anticipates, manages, and resolves conflict in a constructive manner

---

Develops Positive Relationships Assessment Questions

1. Are you known as someone who helps others in the organization?
2. Do you cultivate and share your network?
3. Do you understand and adapt to the various personality styles and working styles within your team?
4. When in conflict situations, how many of the six barriers do you sometimes violate?

The Leader's Toolkit

1. A fun team-building exercise: Understanding Personality Styles Within a Team.

a. Review the characteristics of the four personality styles (Analytical, Driver, Amiable, Expressive) with the group.

b. Create a summary slide or handout with the style descriptors.

c. Clarify that all styles are needed for an effective team. No one style is better than another style.

d. Each team member selects the style that best describes him or her, but does not disclose the style to other team members.

e. Have team members tape a blank piece of paper on their backs. Each team member guesses the style of the other person and writes the style name, along with a few words about why the style was selected, on their team member's paper. For example, Analytical: likes to get into the details.

f. Once everyone has completed the rounds, allow team members to remove the sheet from their back and review, but without comments.

g. Have the group stand in a circle and proceed with the first person: "Sally. What do you think Sally's style is?" The group calls out what style they believe the person is and then the person reveals his or her style.

h. Proceed until everyone's style has been revealed.

2. Build an external networking schedule and commit to have coffee with one new person per week. Ask your new contacts who in their network they would recommend you to meet. Offer to connect them to your network as well. Diagram your network in terms of types of industry, experience, and what help the individuals are seeking. Also, be sure to record the date you met them, as well as a follow-up date.

Chapter 8: Develops Customer Focus

Core Competency: Develops Customer Focus

Develops and sustains productive customer relationships. Gains insight into customer needs and opportunities, and delivers solutions to exceed customer expectations.

Competency Skills
* *Trust and Credibility:* Builds strong internal and external customer relationships by following through on commitments

- *Responsive Problem Solving*: Anticipates and delivers effective and timely solutions to customer problems
- *Needs and Opportunity Awareness*: Proactively identifies opportunities that benefit internal and external customers

Develops Customer Focus Assessment Questions

1. What is your customer's satisfaction score? Do you know the one key change that would improve the score?
2. How are you proactively anticipating and resolving customer problems?
3. What is the lifetime value of one of your key customers?
4. When dealing with customer conflicts, do you treat the person first and then the problem?

The Leader's Toolkit

1. Secret shop your competition and yourself. Review the results with your team and create actions to improve your customer experience. Follow up a few months later by secret shopping yourself again and audit the results—has the customer experience improved?
2. Think about the best customer experience you have had in the past few months. What made the experience exceptional?
   a. Make a list of the elements that you can identify.
   b. Prioritize these elements based on the impact of the elements on your experience.
   c. Compare these elements with your current customer service program and see how you would rate.
   d. Share this exercise with your team.

Chapter 9: Fosters Innovation

Core Competency: Fosters Innovation

Identifies, supports, and champions opportunities for change and continuous improvement. Demonstrates flexibility and adaptability in responding to change and ambiguity.

Competency Skills
- *Change Leadership and Management:* Role models and implements new initiatives effectively within teams and organization
- *Continuous Improvement:* Ongoing effort to develop new and better ideas and new ways of solving problems
- *Complex Thinking:* Adapts approach and develops the best solution to difficult issues involving changes in environment or facts

---

Fosters Innovation Assessment Questions

1. Are you communicating and painting a clear picture of the change and the benefits of the change?
2. How well does your team trust you? How do you know?
3. Great leaders take on the blame and pass on the credit to their team. Are you a great leader?
4. Are you a change agent or someone who is more comfortable with the status quo?
5. Do you encourage new ideas and innovation in others?

The Leader's Toolkit

1. Identify a change that went well. What made this change initiative successful? Now, identify a change in your organization that did not go so well. What were the contributors or learnings from this initiative? For both examples, identify what the key leaders did to support or not support the change.
2. Create a Change Champions group. This is a group of diverse employees from the areas affected by the change. Use this group to obtain input and

feedback about the effectiveness of your communication. The members can offer suggestions about the frequency and messaging of your communication. You may also see this group organically become advocates for the change initiative.

3. Five Stickies

   a. Each group member gets five stickies, or Post-it Notes, and writes one new idea on each of the stickies.

   b. Once members have completed their ideas, divide the group into partners (of two) and direct them to consolidate their ten stickies to five stickies.

   c. Form groups of four and continue the consolidation exercise until you have a manageable number of new ideas to discuss with the large group.

   d. Remember, there are no bad ideas!

   e. Write the outcome of the session on a board where everyone can see it. For example, New Sales Incentive Program.

Chapter 10: Models Personal Growth

Core Competency: Models Personal Growth

Maintains an attitude of open, curious, and proactive learning—continually expanding own area of understanding and expertise. Demonstrates awareness and accurate assessment of personal effectiveness, and practices methods to maintain and generate positive energy through stressful situations.

Competency Skills
- *Self-Awareness:* Clearly understands one's emotions, thoughts, motivations, strengths, and development needs
- *Continuous Learning:* Proactively develops and improve skills and knowledge, never stops learning, and readily volunteers for new projects and challenges
- *Managing Personal Energy and Time:* Establishes rituals and responses to manage personal energy, enabling a greater presence and focus

Models Personal Growth Assessment Questions

1. If you knew you could not fail, what would you be doing differently?

2. What is your mechanism to control or manage your self-sabotage or pessimistic thoughts?

3. Are you continually growing yourself as a leader? What is your personal development plan?

4. Exercise may be the best cure for fatigue. Do you make time for at least 20 minutes of exercise three times a week?

5. Are you spending your time on the most important elements of your life (personal and professional)?

The Leaders Toolkit

1. Leaders and teams need to feel like they have a win, which helps to fuel personal energy. Sometimes, when there are so many conflicting priorities, you do not feel like you are winning or getting anything accomplished. This affects your engagement and energy. Try this exercise to help provide focus and alignment within the team:

   a. Gather your team together first thing in the morning on Monday on a weekly basis.

   b. Have each team member bring the most important project/task he or she must accomplish that week. Each member can only submit one item. (Although we all know that we all have more than one thing we will accomplish during the week, the exercise is meant to bring focus to the most important task.)

   c. Assign a scribe and ensure the scribe notes the name, week, and task that each team member submits for the week.

   d. The following Monday, have each person report on his or her actions and then commit to the current week's actions.

   e. At the end of the team reports, take a couple of minutes to say a few words about the upcoming week—words of appreciation for the hard work, focus, and energy for the upcoming week.

2. Breathe to Calm. Commit to this exercise for at least 1 week and assess how you feel.

   a. Two to three times per day

   b. Find a quiet place, with no cellphone or other distractions.

   c. Close your eyes.

   d. Take ten deep breaths: inhale slowly and deeply, then slowly exhale.

Focus only on the elements of your breathing.

APPENDIX C

Glossary of Financial Terms

In Chapter 4, we discussed the importance of business acumen to being a great manager and leader. We also talked about how understanding how your organization runs and makes money should be important to everyone on your team, not just to the accounting and finance department.

To help educate yourself and your team, review this glossary of financial terms with your team and assign a few key terms to each person (or groups of people for larger teams).

At your next team meeting, have each of person or group present the term and how it specifically applies to your organization. You also may want to invite someone from the finance or accounting department to one of your team meetings to help educate your team on the basic financial terms and how they apply to your organization, the departments they work in, and how their position within the organization affects specific terms.

Asset: Purchased to increase the value of a firm or benefit the firm's operation; can generate cash flow, drive sales, or improve operational efficiency

Business Acumen: Ability to understand how your business operates and makes money, and to proactively anticipate, navigate, and leverage trends affecting your business

Business Driver: Drives and creates the value of a business; various components affecting organizational performance, such as customer service and product offering

Capital Growth: How much an asset has increased in value over a period of time

Cash Generation: Money that an organization can invest after other costs associated with the business have been paid

Cost of Goods Sold: Costs of producing the product that is being sold

Customer Service: Aligning products and service with customer satisfaction; ongoing client relationships that are maintained to continue key revenue

Expense: Cost of doing business; any costs associated with generating or creating revenue

External Factors: Factors outside of a business that have an economic impact on the business, such as the environment, technology, people, and regulations

Gross Profit: Amount of profit generated after cost of goods sold from revenue

Net Income: Total amount of income remaining after the deduction of expenses from revenue

Operating Expenses: Money used to operate a business, including expenses such as salaries, travel, rent, and utilities

Operating Income: Profit from core operations or basic business activities; what is left after the cost of goods sold and operating expenses are deducted from revenues before subtracting additional expenses such as interest and taxes

Return on Investment (ROI): The measurement of how much revenue is generated as it relates to the amount of money invested, calculated by return earned from that investment divided by cost of the investment

Revenue: Money or cash generated by your business as the result of sales, prior to cost or expenses deducted

ABOUT THE AUTHORS

Tammy R. Berberick is president and CEO for Crestcom International. Tammy is a former corporate vice president for a global Fortune 500 company and has held numerous executive-level leadership positions across finance, information technology, human resources, strategy, and sales operations. She has worked as a CPA and business consultant for one of the top global accounting and consulting firms. Tammy was a consultant to CEOs on leadership, change management, organization design, and strategy. She also is committed to giving back to the community and has served on numerous community boards, and also has developed and facilitated a high school leadership program and served as an executive in residence for a graduate-level leadership program. Tammy is passionate about leadership and helping others grow as great leaders.

Peter Lindsay is the director of operations for Crestcom International. He is a former officer in the U.S. Air Force and is a global facilitator in leadership development. Recognized as a thought leader, he is a trainer, instructional designer, and author in leadership and social change. Peter keeps his balance through involvement in a social and humanitarian organization dedicated to advocate for women's and children's rights.

Katie Fritchen is the brand and content strategist for Crestcom International. Katie has worked 6 years in the leadership development field after graduating from the University of Oregon's Lundquist School of Business. She is a writer and editor specializing in business topics, and is author of the upcoming book, *The Millennial's Guide to the Hamster Wheel*. Outside of work, Katie is an avid outdoorswoman and advocates for environmental stewardship through her volunteer work with projects and several nonprofit organizations.

ABOUT CRESTCOM

Crestcom International directs global leadership development initiatives for more than 20,000 organizations in more than 60 countries. With leadership experience spanning 30 years, Crestcom delivers interactive leadership development that produces real results. Crestcom helps leadership teams navigate their key business challenges through in-depth training programs available locally in most parts of the world. Organizations partner with Crestcom for sustainable and measurable leadership results. Every session produces measurable action plans. Every manager implements lasting personal or team improvements. Every team interactively learns practical concepts and tactics, and every chief executive discovers new capacity with existing leaders. Learn more about Crestcom's local training programs, and subscribe to our blog for more advice and insights, by visiting us at www.crestcomleadership.com.

Stay on track with your leadership habit goals by following us:

LinkedIn: www.linkedin.com/company/crestcom-international-llc

Facebook: www.facebook.com/crestcomleadership/

Twitter: @crestcomleaders

Index